THE
BUSINESS
PLAYBOOK

THE BUSINESS PLAYBOOK

How to Document and Delegate What You Do So Your Company Can Grow Beyond You

CHRIS RONZIO

LIONCREST
PUBLISHING

THE BUSINESS PLAYBOOK
How to Document and Delegate What You Do
So Your Company Can Grow Beyond You

ISBN		
	978-1-5445-2415-3	*Hardcover*
	978-1-5445-2413-9	*Paperback*
	978-1-5445-2414-6	*Ebook*

For all the people who say,
"If you want something done right, do it yourself."
I think you're wrong.

CONTENTS

Foreword *ix*

Introduction *1*

The Four Elements of a Playbook *13*

When, Where, How, and Whether to Start *29*

Your Profile:
Defining What Makes Your Business Unique *45*

Your People:
Making the Map for Who's Who and What They Do *73*

Your Policies:
Writing the Rules of Play *93*

Your Processes:
Shifting from "How You Do It" to "How *We* Do It" *113*

Your Playbook in Action *143*

No Playbook Lasts Forever *159*

Conclusion *171*

Acknowledgments *177*

FOREWORD

by Michael E. Gerber

You've probably heard that you need to work on your business, not in it. That's my line and the foundation of my E-Myth books, which millions have read. I came up with the concept after watching countless entrepreneurs struggle to build a business that could actually survive.

How do you develop a sustainable business? My books teach that it's absolutely essential to create and document a system that works. Documentation says, "This is how we do it here."

If you don't *document* your business, you don't *own* it. It just keeps on changing. So how in the world can you possibly replicate who you are, and what you do, and the way that you do it, if you never write it down?

As I often say, chaos produces nothing more than chaos. Without being able to show someone what to do, how to do it, and what it produces—there can be no *consistency*. There can be no *effectiveness*. There can be no *authenticity*, no *control* over what you do. And there can be no *growth*.

For Chris Ronzio, who devoured my books, the documentation idea inspired questions he dedicated years to answering for himself and for every other small-business owner/entrepreneur: *How* do you document your business? How do you create a *playbook* for it?

He searched, experimented, and fine-tuned until he had practical answers. Then he poured them into this book—with magnificent precision to a degree never accomplished before.

The system *is* the solution to your small business's survival. Thanks to Chris, you now hold that system in your hands.

Read it, believe it, *use* it—don't put off working on your playbook a moment longer—and you'll reap enormous rewards for your business...and your life. Because you won't just make a living; you'll succeed in making a *difference*.

And isn't that why you started your business in the first place?

INTRODUCTION

I was sick of saving the day. No matter how high-level I tried to remain in my first business (an event video-production company), every time something fell apart—someone would get sick, mess up, or quit—I was thrown back into the mix.

On one particular day, everything came to a head. It was the holidays, and I had plans with my family, but those plans were about to blow up. I found out at 7 p.m. that our crew for the next day was canceled...in Los Angeles. I had to leave right away to make the six-hour drive from Phoenix, Arizona. The equipment shop agreed to open for me at 6 a.m. so I could rent a camera, replace the crew, and save the day once again.

At the event and on the long drive home, I was exhausted, frustrated, and miserable. I thought, "This is not what I signed up for. I can't do this forever. It doesn't *scale*." Call it an epiphany, but I knew then that something major had to change.

I know you can relate; spreading ourselves too thin is the universal experience of entrepreneurs. It feels like we can blame the problem on time. We want our businesses to scale, but the way it seems to scale is by working eight, then twelve, then even sixteen and twenty hours a day. Why?

It's *not* that you can't afford some help, so what's really sucking you in?

The *real* problem is that you keep your business, and everything about how it runs, locked up inside your head. You're the only one who knows how the wheels turn. That's also why you find it much too stressful to hand off the reins to anyone else—you're convinced they won't do things the way you would.

But you should also know you can't keep up this pace. Everyone has limits, and you don't want to wait until you or your relationships *break* to find yours. So it's a good thing you found this book first—maybe just in time.

The only way to get out of this unhealthy cycle is to create a playbook—a living document that gets your business out of your brain and into a structure you can share with the reliable people who work for you. The playbook fills the knowledge gap by letting you build a business that doesn't rely on you to keep it going every day. It allows your business to run without you. It lets you take a holiday off (or even a vacation!) and come back to results that meet or exceed your expectations. You can scale without losing sleep. It's not just a dream; it's *doable*.

If someday you decide to sell, a playbook helps you there, too. It makes your business that much more attractive because a potential buyer knows they can hit the ground running. They can feel confident that the business will survive in their hands.

This book shows you everything you need to create the playbook your business needs.

WHY I'M THE ONE TO HELP YOU

I wrote *The Business Playbook* because I've gone through every stage in the process we talk about in this book, both directly and indirectly.

In it, I lay out the principles and structures I've learned throughout my career, starting with those chaotic times when not having a playbook cost me—a *lot*. Without a playbook, I had been hiring friends, or friends of friends, who lost too much in the translation when they learned on the job, so they weren't prepared to handle inevitable emergencies like the loss of power in the arena or irrationally disgruntled customers. If you don't have instructions, you at least need to hire experienced people. I had neither, and that was a recipe for disaster.

After my epiphany during that unplanned "holiday" trip to California, I knew what I had to do: streamline my training process and build a database of fully trained camera operators and sales reps who know the business and are ready to go when something comes up.

"Streamline" was relative back then. I hobbled together a concoction of four systems: a password-protected Word-Press website, a sequence of emailed training videos, a quiz, and a customer relationship management (CRM) system that would track training status and enter contact info in our database. It was messy, but it was enough to solve my problem.

My team wasted no time finding crews in cities across the US (within a five-hour drive of any possible event location to cut down on flights) and training them through our new online system. When a job came up in a certain city, we could just ping that list and give the job to the first person who responded. Staffing production suddenly became so much easier. I no longer missed holidays, and my company wasn't the only one to benefit: the freelance operators I contracted also loved our business model because they could be trained in advance and be on call for on-demand events.

But there was no getting around the fact that the process was convoluted. I started to form a mental vision of doing it all with just one beautiful system, not that I would get around to actually creating one for years.

For the time being, I had solved our operations problem and reached optimum efficiency for the business, so within three years, I was ready to sell it. My other reason for selling was a new problem that was facing me: It was 2010, a time when smartphones with HD cameras were beginning to find their way into every parent's back pocket, so they were less in need of our professional coverage.

It wasn't long before my next venture found me.

The process of organizing my company had made me a ninja of operational workflows—I lived to be superefficient. Through the lens of my company, other people's businesses looked wildly disorganized. Members of my entrepreneurs' group started asking me to visit and tell them what they could do better. I loved learning about different businesses and applying the streamlined process that had worked so well at my former company: I'd study their operations, interview their people, map out the workflow, and recommend tech tools to make their processes run efficiently.

This consulting pastime grew into my second company, called Organize Chaos, which ultimately helped 150 businesses to clean up their operations and become more productive.

Around the same time, I volunteered to mentor student entrepreneurs through a program at Arizona State University. One group of three engineers had come up with an HR onboarding tool for large enterprise companies. A year later, when a client of mine needed help with a big turnover issue, I reached out to those students to see if their onboarding tool could help. They'd finished school and the project by then, so they were happy to sell me the code. I engaged contract developers to turn it into my vision for a product that would help small, growing companies document their policies and processes online. That became the first version of Trainual, launched in January 2015.

Over the three years that followed, I used that software with my consulting clients. When I decided to scale that company beyond just me, I also used the product to train the consultants I hired. As I did, it became clear that this software thing might turn out to be more scalable than consulting. I hired a full-time developer and, by 2018, we had launched Trainual version 2.

We also started Trainual Inc, the company, to sell the software and share the learning that my team and I had gained by helping hundreds of businesses to streamline their operations.

WHAT YOU'LL GET FROM THIS BOOK

You've probably learned the hard way that when you're the only one who knows what you know about the business, you can't get other people up and running quickly. Every owner I've talked to wants the same thing: an efficient workflow that makes sense to everyone in the company. They—and you, no doubt—want to be able to trust the operation of their business to someone else. Wouldn't it be great to hand it over without a hiccup (or worse) and work fewer hours, so you can take a break now and then?

This book will show you how to get your systems and processes written down and shareable. All of that knowledge is so much a part of you that you take it for granted—right up until the time the roof falls in because you can't be reached. Having a playbook that includes everything that makes your business *your business* allows it to exist beyond you. It allows you to take a step back from the day-to-day to get more time for whatever you'd rather be doing.

No matter who ultimately takes on that day-to-day, building a playbook gets you thinking about how to successfully onboard your people so they understand what they need to know and when they need to know it. Of all the benefits of a playbook, creating a standard onboarding process is the one that means the most to many of our customers. At the same time, you'll be shaping a culture that values process and efficiency, as well as gaining in all the other ways you'll learn about in Chapter 1.

This book is a guide and a recipe for the what, who, how, when, and why of building your company's playbook and making it stick. Having one and keeping it up-to-date are without a doubt the best ways to streamline and organize your business. But it won't write itself. There's no template that applies to every business because no two businesses are exactly the same. Reading this book is easy; creating the playbook will take commitment.

That commitment will be worth your time if you own or help lead a company you want to grow. On the other hand, if you reject the idea that anyone will ever be better at what you do than you are and you're content to keep the work to yourself forever, I recommend finding something else to read. A business playbook, let alone this book about making one, won't do a thing for you.

This book also won't do you any good if your whole business runs on automation rather than people because, well, you don't have anyone to train. But if you have a people-powered business—if you like the idea of creating a community in your company and supporting careers and other families— this book will help you build that foundation, a foundation for everyone to succeed.

The playbook is for people with "small" businesses, not that I'm comfortable defining that maximum. I *can* tell you that it's for a company where the owner or owners are *still* involved in the company because if they're no longer involved, chances are, a playbook was already created.

I can also be clear about a *minimum* business size and relative stage that the book will benefit: you need a business that's no longer in its infancy or struggling to find its next customer. You also likely have a handful of people and some division of departments to lay the groundwork for all the other roles you'll hire. If you're focusing on how to consistently support more customers while maintaining quality, it's time for a playbook.

Before we go any further, let me point out that this book is also for you if your "company" is a school, a nonprofit, a local government, or some other description of a business entity. I've used the words "company" and "business" throughout to represent whatever you do for work.

Whatever that is, don't playbook prematurely, though. If you're a solo technician so far, wait until you're ready to start shedding and delegating some of your responsibilities before taking on the task. Focus on what you could delegate. And, if you're perfectly content doing it all yourself, there's probably no need for a playbook.

HOW TO WORK WITH THIS BOOK

I recommend that you read the book all the way through the first time and then share it with your key team members as a whole or in parts. Because creating a playbook is a team sport and an ongoing effort, I've designed each chapter to support that collaboration by being able to stand alone. For example, when you ask a team member to write the part of the playbook that covers their responsibilities, in Chapter 4, they'll find advice, formatting tips, and exercises to help them document the section they're working on. And each of the four "Elements" chapters (3 through 6) ends with a useful checklist.

DO IT.
DOCUMENT IT.
DELEGATE IT.®

The chapters generally follow a three-step process that demonstrates the maturity of a business or any role or task you do in it. We at Trainual refer to this process as Do It. Document It. Delegate It.® Here's how it works:

At the start of the business, when you're just coming up with your list of products or services, you're not sure what's going to work until you test everything with real customers. As you get more and more feedback, you can adjust and refine your offering. Over time, you developed a repeatable method that gives you the best consistent results. That's the "Do It" part—the work you need to do before you can create a playbook, and you'll find it in Chapter 2.

Chapters 3 through 6 are all about how to "Document It"— creating the playbook by writing down or recording the various areas of your business so that you can communicate them to another person.

Chapter 7 will show you how to "Delegate It"—the responsibilities—and how to implement the playbook throughout your company, including your team now and in the future.

(In addition, there's a chapter to introduce the elements of a playbook—the following one—and Chapter 8, about when and how to update your playbook.)

COMING UP

Now that you know exactly why you're here, it's time to start thinking about the project in front of you. The first step is knowing exactly what goes into a business playbook. In the next chapter, I'll pull back the curtain on its DNA.

1

THE FOUR ELEMENTS
OF A PLAYBOOK

W hile I was a freshman in high school, I started a video-production company with a friend of mine. It started off casually, recording anything someone would pay us to record: weddings, bar mitzvahs, music videos, commercials, and my neighbor's cousin's grandfather's ninetieth birthday party.

Eventually, we got our big break: visiting state administrators saw us carrying camera gear around the high-school gym and asked us to film the following weekend's state cheerleading competition. In exchange for our services, they said we could set up a table at the event to take video orders from the competitors' parents.

Of course, we were ecstatic about the opportunity and immediately agreed. I took the orders while my friend ran the camera. That weekend, we made more than $900, the most cash I'd ever laid my hands on. We spread the money out all over my bed as if we had hit the lottery. I felt like Scrooge McDuck; we couldn't *believe* our good fortune. Our little company was on its way.

Twice a year for ten years, we shot and sold videos for this event while we took on more complicated events for other organizations. As our productions got more complicated, we began documenting the difficult processes and best practices, like the best loading dock at each arena, how to boost the signal on a 1,000-ft. cable run, and the camera with the best battery life, to use where there was no AC power. We didn't do the same for the cheerleading event, though, because after all those years, it had become second nature. A simple email exchange with our friends at the state office was all the prep we needed.

Everything went well...until the year it didn't. That was when we finally hired an event coordinator, one month before the championship. I had moved to Arizona and into less involvement with the business operations. On the morning of the event, I got a frantic set of texts from its host saying, "Where are you guys?"

Nooooo!

Panic set in. I suddenly realized that although we had trained our new event coordinator in the complex stuff, we had left out the event we'd never documented because we took it for granted. We had completely messed up.

That morning, there was no video for the event, no video on the Jumbotron, no video to give the judges for their technical replays—no record of each child's important state championship for parents to buy and grandparents around the world to livestream. We felt horrible.

Of course, we lost the contract, and not long after, the employee, who quit because of stress; although we didn't blame her for the incident, we also never set her up for success. The experience made this fact abundantly clear: institutional knowledge does not scale a business.

It also highlighted an important lesson that came out of that fact: if we had put more time and effort into documenting our events, and if we had shared that documentation with our event coordinator as part of her training, that disaster would not have happened.

It often takes an emergency to spark the urgency to create a playbook. Don't let it happen to you: create the playbook to *avoid* emergencies. First, you need to know exactly what it is, what goes into it, and all the reasons it can help you.

Create a *what?*

By business playbook, I mean a collection and record of the experience, knowledge, and structure of your business. It's what makes your business unique. Like snowflakes, no two playbooks are alike because no two businesses are either— even within the same industry. In fact, there's only one thing playbooks do have in common, and that's the structure you'll fill in with your business's specifics.

Those specifics begin with your company's profile: your culture, your brand, and your spot in the market. They also include who does what, how they do it, and the rules or policies that guide it.

The playbook collects *internal* knowledge—the ingredients in your special sauce, your company's DNA: it's everything you experience and learn from the inside of your business, like who your ideal customers are and how to make them happy.

External knowledge, on the other hand, does *not* belong in the playbook. You can get that anywhere. It is the stuff you learn at the same time as your competitors—news articles you read, courses you take, conferences you attend.

Think of a couple of surgeons who collect the same external knowledge by going to the same medical school, sitting through the same classes, and getting the same degree and certification. It's not until they go out in the world and work for different hospital systems that everything—like procedures, policies, checklists, and systems—changes.

As with hospitals, your business's internal knowledge is different from others'. Those differences are exactly why you need a playbook. It's also why no playbook comes as one-size-fits-all or even one-size-fits-*anyone*-else. You might think of it as a custom course you create to show the people you choose how to run or take over your business.

Along with internal knowledge, your playbook should focus on the highest layers of priority. So you'll need to make a clear distinction between what's *required*—the stuff your staff has to understand and sign off on, what they need to do their jobs, and how to operate within the company—versus what's *reference*, or the optional stuff to look up later if and when they need it.

You're not creating a textbook or an "education" with your playbook. You never want to burden someone with too much information. Not only would it create a bad experience for employees, it would distract from what they really need to learn.

WHY ELSE YOU NEED A PLAYBOOK

There are *so* many reasons to document what you do. Let's focus on the most important ones, a mix of emotional and practical:

Unburden yourself. You might find that the playbook's biggest value is getting the business out of your head and into a shareable form because of the weight it takes off your shoulders. It gives you the gift of time you can spend any way you like.

Establish consistently high standards. Guard against things getting out of hand as your business grows and you hire multiple people for the same roles. With even only two people doing the same job, you'll start to notice differences in performance. For example, early on at Trainual, a dozen people put their own spin on their web presentation to prospective customers and saw vastly different close and conversion rates. It was not until we streamlined and documented the most successful presentation into the playbook that we could ensure the same experience for each prospect.

Enhance the *employee* experience in four ways. When you start a business, all of your energy goes towards the *customer's* experience. As the business grows enough to hire people, your focus should shift to include them, too.

- **Orienting:** A playbook shows what's expected of new team members and how their careers can grow.

- **Sharing skills:** You invest in your team's career advancement when your senior people pass along what they've learned to junior ones.

- **Creating backups:** Any business that's mature enough to offer benefits and support people should have a plan for sick days, parental leave, and other days off. That means cross-training: having at least one extra person who knows how to do every job, so any time the primary person takes leave, you don't have to panic; your business won't miss a beat.

- **Building in alignment:** You'll also realize the benefit of keeping your business and employees aligned on vision and core values. Creating a playbook can provide the motivation to get those straight.

Generate a valuable asset. Good for you and your employees. If you could choose between buying and renting a house and you had the money, wouldn't you buy? Then you'd have an *asset.* Well, the real asset of your company is the collective experience and knowledge you and your team have gained through being in business. If you're not capturing that experience and knowledge in a playbook, paying salaries becomes like paying rent—you have nothing permanent to show for all of that effort.

What's more, if someone else—an employee or the next owner—can't take over and operate the business the same way you would, your business isn't worth much. By keeping the business's daily operations from depending on you, the playbook increases your company's value.

WHAT'S IN YOUR PLAYBOOK

Like the elements in the periodic table, the elements of a playbook are universal. *Unlike* the periodic table's 118 elements, a playbook has only four (each starting with the letter "P" for playbook). I'll go into detail about each one in upcoming chapters, but here's a preview:

The first element is your **Profile**—similar to a profile on social media, the company profile on your playbook is how you introduce what your business is about. It includes your brand, culture, values, mission, vision, and history. The profile section also explains to new hires or potential investors/acquirers why you exist, who you serve, basically how you serve them, and how you differ from other businesses in the same category.

The second element is the **People** who work in the business—a matter of intense curiosity for new hires. They're already looking everyone up on LinkedIn to get a feel for who they'll interact with; they'll appreciate it if you put everything in one place for them. This element helps everyone understand who's who, and who does what in your company.

Third is your company's **Policies**—the operating rules and standards that would typically go into an employee handbook. They include everything from office-access hours, dress code, and vacation time to legal compliance: state and federal regulations, and anti-harassment and safety information. (Start with the policies that apply to everyone.)

The final element is **Process**—the "plays" part of the playbook. It's my favorite element: while Profile, People, and Policies make up the foundation of the building, Processes help you grow into a skyscraper because they scale your business's capacity to produce. They result in more people delivering more products and services to more customers, and doing it consistently. Processes are the step-by-step, start-to-finish sequences of accomplishing a task or meeting a responsibility inside a business. Documenting them leads to being most efficient, and, of course, efficiency leads to profits.

Process is also the playbook section that always takes the most time and requires the most frequent updating.

This process element is where most people are tempted to begin the playbook, probably because so many business books recommend creating operations manuals and standard operating procedures (also referred to as SOPs). But I recommend that you save it for last—*after* describing your expectations for new hires—because it's the last thing your new hires need to know. "What," "who," "why," and "when" all come before "how." For one thing, they need to understand the business, the people they'll work with, and the rules of the workplace before they get into the complexities of their job. If you start with the process instead, you risk looking like you're micromanaging people with your playbook rather than empowering them.

Still another reason to leave the process section for the end is because you'll get the most ROI from starting with and focusing on what will impact the most people. Everyone who works for your business, no matter what their job, needs to understand the profile of the business, the people they'll work with, and the policies that apply to them. Processes, on the other hand, need to get granular, because in many cases, only one person will do each of them. As you move through the elements, the ROI diminishes as each gets less and less relevant to the entire team.

THE SEVEN ESSENTIAL QUALITIES OF A SUCCESSFUL PLAYBOOK

You won't get credit and value from just any series of documents you collect into something you call a playbook. For it to accomplish the benefits mentioned in this chapter, your playbook needs to demonstrate some key characteristics.

Your playbook must be **accessible**. Photographers like to say that the best camera is the one you have on you—without a camera, you have no picture. The same applies to your playbook. If people can't get to it when they need it, you might as well not bother. Your playbook has to live online, where everyone who ever needs it can access it wherever they are, from any device.

The information in it must be **searchable**. Unlike software designed to teach a curriculum and test on retention, a playbook needs to enable people to find answers quickly. Consider searchability when you're choosing your playbook platform. It's hard to search through more than just the titles of hundreds of Word documents or through many learning-management systems from which some businesses start documenting. By contrast, wikis or knowledge bases facilitate searching.

Another essential quality for your business's playbook is to be **collaborative**. Big companies often have a department that creates training for everyone in them. But effective playbooks for small businesses develop as the result of a bottom-up, not top-down, approach. That's because there's rarely any one person who understands every aspect of a business. So, everyone should participate and create the part of the playbook that covers what they do.

Your playbook should be **instructive**, actually explaining concepts and not just listing tasks. You won't just *look* like you're micromanaging if your playbook is a checklist and you force people to check off every item each time they do the process when they've already learned it. Learning is different from doing; your playbook should teach a set of skills that, once learned, leaves people alone to just perform them.

That's a lesson I could have used in my video company. When we boiled down the hundreds of minute tasks for every single event we produced, loaded them into a project-management system, and assigned them to team members based on their role, we thought we had done an awesome job.

But as we did more and more events, some people ended up with thousands of assigned tasks to check off—tasks that they already knew how to do. It became a burden, the opposite of what a playbook should do, which is to give people only needed instruction on assignments, then to trust them to do their jobs.

Your playbook must be **fluid**, never one-and-done. The playbook you have today should not be the one you have next year, or maybe even next month. It should be easy to update on the fly because it needs to change as often as your business introduces more products and services, hires more people, and comes up with new best practices.

Where paper, wikis, and checklists can be a daunting blank slate, a playbook is **structured**. Your playbook has concrete sections (the elements), and an organized way to introduce each of them that you can easily create. Similar to lessons within courses, a playbook also has a sequence to it—a guided experience.

Finally, and most importantly, a playbook is **trackable**. You should have a way to hold your team accountable for the knowledge that you assign to them. Assigning and tracking your playbook is the two-way feedback loop that ensures alignment and understanding, so that what you document can be followed by all.

Here is a look at how all of the different categories stack up against one another:

I can't help but recommend Trainual here (and not just because it's my company!). Borrowing from other formats, the software blends the searchability of a wiki, the ease of

	Accessible	Searchable	Collaborative	Instructive	Fluid	Structured	Trackable
Paper Manuals & Binders				✓			
Online Docs & Sheets	✓		✓	✓	✓		
Wikis & Knowledge Bases	✓	✓	✓	✓	✓		
Checklists & Task Mgmt	✓	✓	✓		✓		✓
Course Authoring	✓			✓	✓	✓	✓
Learning Management	✓			✓		✓	✓
Playbooks	✓	✓	✓	✓	✓	✓	✓

use of a Word document, the accountability and tracking of the learning-management software, and the collaborative features of Google Docs. We then overlaid the structure that businesses operate on to create dedicated playbook software.

THE POWER OF A PLAYBOOK

I'll never forget the disappointment and shame I felt when my video company's long-term great relationship with our first client fell apart because we didn't take the time to train our newest hire. We had failed to explain her role and tasks and failed to give her the resources she needed from the get-go. If we had only documented everything, we wouldn't have let down an organization who'd put their trust in us early on.

Now that you've learned what a playbook can do for your business and the risks of not having one, such a disaster doesn't ever have to happen to you. You also have seen that everything in your business fits into one of a playbook's four buckets, and you'll soon find out exactly how.

At this point, I hope you're raring to go—but hold off before you start documenting. To avoid wasting your time and to create a playbook that works for your business, you first need to figure out whether your business is *ready* for a playbook and what to take care of first if it isn't. In the next chapter, you'll get the details.

2

WHEN, WHERE, HOW, AND WHETHER TO START

A former client of mine is a wholesale real estate investor who bought and flipped properties that had to sell quickly, whether because of a code violation, a probate situation, or fire damage. They would make offers on the properties so they could build up the company's portfolio. Then they would fix them up themselves or sell them to other wholesale investors. That was their niche, and they had successfully operated that way in the West Phoenix area for a decade.

Around that point, the company wanted to expand beyond their familiar territory, and they called me in to help. To give them the big picture—a vision of their business at scale—I mapped out the multistage process of closing deals. I was happy to brainstorm the systems that could help them handle hundreds of real estate transactions around the world. But I advised them to start small and learn each new market one at a time.

They didn't take my advice. They were so desperate for growth that they built this expansion from scratch rather than scale what was already working. They hired a dozen assistants to place calls to buy properties in states beyond Arizona, wrote a script, and created a training program to document and share what they *thought* would work. Within a matter of weeks, the company leaders felt like they had built this nationwide operation that couldn't possibly lose.

After two months, though, it was a whole different story: pure frustration. They were spending a lot of money and not closing any deals. Three months in, they had to pull the plug on their grand plans. They let the new phone team go and scrapped the training.

They thought they had done everything right! They had written down all of the knowledge they expected they'd need to start buying properties outside of Phoenix. But those expectations were way off because they didn't know those markets. They hadn't shown any success in them, so they were not capable of training their assistants or documenting that training for the future.

At the same time that they were scaling, they were actually building a new business from scratch. That's not how you do it. It's just one example of what happens almost every time someone tries to create written standards for processes or any other instructions without taking the time to prove that the processes actually work. It's like creating an empty playbook instead of documenting one that's proven.

It took failing for the company to realize they needed to go back to what they're good at, which was *not* building a call center of remote assistants trying to close deals in unfamiliar locations around the world. It was negotiating deals on damaged property.

Maybe you too are still experimenting with your business model, your market, and your products and services, and deciding on the roles and responsibilities inside the company. If that's the case, as I mentioned in the previous chapter, creating a playbook is not your logical next step to success. It's still a few steps down the road.

Your first business priority should be to create something that works—first with one customer, then with ten or more. Before you can document and scale, you need consistent, battle-tested processes. You shouldn't *write* the way to do it until there's a *right* way to do it.

Think of your playbook like a cookbook: you wouldn't share the recipe until you've finished experimenting with it. Figure out what you need to focus on and get right first. The playbook will be here when you're ready.

WHAT TO GET RIGHT FIRST

To help you decide whether your business is ready for a playbook, look closely and objectively at your business and answer these questions:

Is your business mature enough? It might be if you have at least some separation of roles and responsibilities. But it's definitely not mature enough for a playbook if only one person is doing every job.

Do you want a playbook for the right reasons? What's a bigger problem for your business: Is it getting more customers? Or is it being able to consistently and efficiently deliver to the customers you are already getting? (Hint: if you and your team are working too many hours trying to catch up on fulfilling orders or if you need to offload some of your workload, that's a good sign you need a playbook.)

The first—getting more customers—is a *revenue* problem, and as you saw with our real estate client, a playbook can't solve that. If that's what you're dealing with, spend your time and energy working on marketing and sales.

Delivery is an *operations* problem, which a playbook *does* solve. Documenting repeatable processes enables you to scale and meet the demand. (Scaling your operations also happens to grow revenue, but only as a by-product of a much more streamlined business.)

Why else do you want a playbook? Maybe you plan to sell the business. Or you want to create a better work–life balance; instead of continuing to allow the business to dominate your life, you want to be able to take a vacation now and then or spend more time with your family. Maybe you aspire to open multiple locations or develop a franchise. Or you might want to pass along the hands-on part of your business to free up your time for your next venture. Keep your answer to "why" in mind for when we talk about how to enlist the help of your team.

Is your team ready and willing to get behind your vision? Regardless of your rationale for building your playbook, if you don't have a good relationship with your people, you'll find it hard or impossible to get them on board. Never start work on a playbook before you're confident that you'll get their help and support—even their excitement.

You're the boss, so you might wonder why you need to take time to gain their buy-in, rather than assigning their participation with no preparation. Well, just take a moment to imagine how they would react if you were to spring on them that they need to write down everything they do. They're likely to feel panic, even paranoid: "Are you trying to get rid of me?" "If I write down everything, why do you need me?" "Are you going to hire someone to do my job for less money?" "Are we downsizing or shutting down?" "Do I need to find another job?"

I saw that reaction face-to-face when I worked with a luxury moving and storage company client to improve their warehouse-inventory systems. I conducted confidential interviews with each team member to find out what they did. A back-office administrator walked into the room, sat down, looked me up and down then square in the face, and said, "I'm not telling you *anything.*"

My reaction was to gasp; I couldn't believe she said that to me in our first interaction ever. Then she pointed at my pocket and the thin wire hanging out of it. She said, "You're *wired*; you're recording all of this, so I'm not going to tell you anything." After I suppressed my laughter, I showed her and explained: "This is my insulin pump. I've had type 1 diabetes since I was a little kid. These interviews *are* confidential."

With that explanation, she agreed to proceed (*without* snipping the wire), but the example shows how easy it is for someone to fear for their job when they don't understand why you're asking them to lay it out for you. Until I witnessed that fear, I didn't know I needed to communicate with the employees in advance. Lesson learned: that experience taught me never again to leave employees to draw their own frightening conclusions. After that, I always sent ahead an information sheet about my process and purpose.

HOW TO PREPARE YOUR TEAM FOR THE PLAYBOOK PROJECT

Be strategic about how you break the news: if your company is small enough to fit in one room, a preview in an all-hands meeting might help you get ahead of questions and concerns. For a bigger company, you might choose to send out a video or an email, something like this sample:

One Way to Get the Team Onboard

Hi, everyone!

We're working on building a playbook for [company name] so that we can [list reasons for building it].

Shortly you'll be receiving a Trainual [or insert any other system] invite to organize your responsibilities, share more about yourself, and document your own best practices to contribute to making our business better.

Thanks in advance for your participation, and let me know if you have any questions.

Thanks,

[your name]

If you have a larger company, you've probably already shared your one- or three-year plan with your team. In that case, in your all-hands meeting, you can introduce the playbook as a crucial step to those goals, saying something that fits your situation. For example:

Remember when we had that meeting about opening a third location in twelve months? This playbook is one of the ways we'll do it. I learned there are inconsistencies between our first two locations, so during the first half of the year, we'll all put our heads together and refine and establish our best practices into the playbook. Thank you for helping with that. I'll follow up with each of you to talk about your specific role, but I wanted to let you know today that it's coming.

HOW TO FOLLOW UP
ONE-ON-ONE

It's best to personalize these communications, so each person will understand the benefits they themselves will realize when they write down what they know. You might frame the conversation in career-path terms, something like this (mixed and matched depending on who you're talking to):

> If you'll share your best practices, we can hire someone to take some of those tasks off your plate and free you up for higher-level work, which we can pay you more for. How would you feel about that?

Or, if they love what they're doing:

> Wouldn't comparing notes with other people who do the same thing help to make all of you even better at it? That way, you can earn more commissions or get more done in the same amount of time and even leave early some days.

If you do have plans to sell the business after you scale it (or you just want to work less), be transparent with your team about that, too.

Not only does a playbook *not* lead to *cutting* people, it often helps the existing team to become more efficient and delay the company's need to hire more people. But if you have an employee who remains skeptical and resists the playbook process even after your careful explanations, that reaction might signal someone who isn't a long-term fit for the business.

WHERE TO START DOCUMENTING

Now that you've nipped your team's fear in the bud, it's time to work on yours. Avoid letting the playbook project daunt you by having a plan to tackle it in the right order, starting with what gives you the highest ROI on your time investment.

There are a few ways to think about ROI and where to start: by the number of people affected, by the frequency that something is done, and by the consistency of how it needs to be done.

What needs to be known by all? Think of the project from the perspective of a new employee. Every-person that you bring on needs to learn the things that apply to everyone in the company and then what applies to their department (like tools, communication styles, and norms) or, in the case of different locations, their geographic area. Beyond and below that should come the things that apply to just their team, their role, or only them. The fewer people who need to know something, the longer you should wait to document it.

Starting wide helps to reinforce your team's understanding of the value of the playbook in a way that something narrow would not.

What is done most often? For example, in my first business, that task was packaging and mailing DVDs, so it was the first process we documented. If our interns didn't get it right, the very frequency of the task would've created a massive negative impact across the business.

What is done by the most people? Perhaps start with something that requires consistency from one operator to the next, especially if it's what your company is known for. That might come in handy for, say, a team of real estate agents. Each might not sell many houses every year, but because the agency wants to offer consistent service, it should be one of the first things to take up residence in the playbook.

HOW MUCH OF YOUR BUSINESS TO DOCUMENT

It's not realistic to expect that your playbook will make your business so turnkey that it'll run like an assembly line. (That is, unless your business already *is* an assembly line!) Don't try to document everything—limit to the consistent, static things, which should make up 50–80 percent of your business. Technology and best practices change so quickly that if 100 percent of your business is static, it's unlikely to be around long.

That's not to say your playbook won't ever need to change. It will (and we'll talk about *how* towards the end of this book). But the part that's not documented is your space for innovation—the space where you're still "doing it."

In the next four chapters, you'll get suggestions for the topics to document that apply to each of the four Ps.

HOW TO DOCUMENT SOMETHING

When you write down the information about your business for your playbook, keep in mind that you're capturing what already exists. You're not making anything up from scratch. Remembering that you're being an observer and a listener, not a creator, should keep you and your staff from feeling overwhelmed by the process.

Sometimes people are so skilled in a task that it becomes automatic to them. They may struggle to put themselves in the beginner's mind and forget a step when they're training someone or documenting the task. So you might find it useful to pair people up. Get someone who doesn't know the task to watch and interview the person doing it: "What's that button you just hit? And what does it do?" "What button? Oh—that one!" Alternatively, record them doing the task.

What format should you use? The best documentation method, especially at first, is the one that's the easiest for you and your team to produce. Instead of getting hung up on sophisticated formats, put your focus into collecting and organizing the information. You can always improve on the format after you put it in practice.

Later, you can take advantage of multiple formats that tell the story at hand in the clearest, most logical way. For simple instructions, that's probably a numbered list. Other types of "lessons" might lend themselves more to screenshots, videos, audios, text, and still photos, or slide presentations. For example, you'll probably be better off with screenshots to demonstrate a process done on a computer. We'll get into detail in the next four chapters.

Appoint a Project Owner

Even though everyone in your company will contribute, someone needs to be in charge of getting your playbook written. Like any strategic goal, the playbook needs a champion—someone to keep it SMART (specific, measurable, attainable, relevant, and time-based).

That person tends to be someone in an operational or administrative role. If you're not going to be the one at the helm of the playbook, consider who in your company would be best at creating a plan, assigning the sections (again, based on highest ROI), and checking on everyone's progress. Without someone like that, the project is almost certain to get off track.

Allocate Enough Time

Speaking of progress, you might want to know how long your playbook might take from the time you start until you roll out the first draft. A solid quarter (three months) is a realistic minimum timeline to make real progress on a playbook. But if you have a lot to document or you want a first pass that feels closer to finished (not that a playbook is ever finished!), double that time.

Ready to Start?

Just as no one builds a highway unless there's enough traffic to justify it, don't install systems in your business until you create the traffic. Only when my real estate client returned to their roots were they able to document what they're good at and take it to scale.[1]

But if instead of generating traffic, the problem you have to solve is the infrastructure to support more traffic, you're ready to start documenting your business and building your playbook. The next four chapters show you how.

Even thinking about documenting your business forces you to see it as it actually is, as if you're looking at it through

---

1 In fact, they turned what they're good at into a mastermind group for clients. Now they have hundreds of investors around the country who pay them to learn how to negotiate fire-damage deals. And just last week, as I write this, and four years after the company saw the light, the CEO texted me a picture of a six-figure check they'd received from one job that represented an opportunity that came up because they're staying in their lane.

a camera's magnifying lens. You now know to make sure that lens shows you a sound business model with proven success.

Every company's story is different from the millions of other businesses in the world. In the next chapter, you'll learn how to unpack yours for everyone who needs to know it.

3

YOUR PROFILE: DEFINING WHAT MAKES YOUR BUSINESS UNIQUE

f you went to college, think back to the days before you ever set foot on campus. You might have felt more than a little lost. Maybe you worried about not knowing anyone or how to get around. Everything was strange and probably a little scary.

At least that's how I felt as I headed into my own college experience. There I was, fresh out of high school. I didn't know what to expect. I was excited—but also completely intimidated.

Fortunately, only the excitement lasted. That's because my school had put together a three-day orientation for incoming freshmen to visit the campus during the summer, try out the dorms, get to know each other, and most importantly, get a taste of what the next four years would be like.

I went from feeling like a timid kid being dropped off at kindergarten for the first time to feeling like an informed grown-up in charge of my future. By the end of the long weekend, which flew by, this place had turned into my home away from home. I'd made friends, and I'd learned how to swipe my meal card, find my classes, rent space at the library, and a lot of other things that could have caused me a lot of stress if I'd have waited until classes began.

Those three days gave me a chance to kick the tires and get myself up to speed. And already in my school sweatshirt and hat, I had taken on the college brand. I couldn't wait to come back to school a month later.

As an employer, you have the opportunity to create that type of warm experience for every new person that you invite into your company. From the moment they think about applying, they want to understand the culture of your business and whether it's the right fit for them.

While they engage with you in both your interviews and your orientation process, they're looking at whether their first impressions were right.

The best way you can prepare your new hires for what's to come is with the first of the four main playbook elements. That's your company profile—its cultural and contextual representation to the world. It's the story of what makes your business unique.

A profile has the ability to make your new hires feel welcome, quickly oriented, and grounded in everything they need to know to have a successful start in your company. The profile gives every new hire the same experience—an essential foundation and overview on which to overlay the details of their job as they learn them.

By capturing all of the elements that make your company what it is, you'll be able to tell your story consistently to everyone you want to get excited about your business—not only new hires, by the way, but also employees, interns, contractors, volunteers, investors, and future owners.

There's a formula for telling your story consistently and compellingly, and you're about to learn it.

THE PROFILE FORMULA

A number of items belong in the profile—the first section of your playbook. Here they are, in their most logical order.

Say Hello

A warm welcome is the best way to begin that section. Although it may sound obvious, give your newcomers a soft landing by starting with a simple hello. Give every new person the same enthusiastic prerecorded greeting to get them excited about working with you and the process to come. Consistency is important because as your business grows, it may not be possible to have face time with all of your new people due to your schedule, multiple locations, or even an unexpected sick day.

My welcome message is as simple as this:

> Welcome to Trainual! We're excited you're here. The fact that you're watching this video means we like you a lot. A lot of people did not make it through the application process—we hire fewer than 2 percent of the people who apply. It's harder to get into Trainual than Harvard, so you must be pretty special.

Over the next few days you're going to learn a lot about us. If you have questions at any point, please ask. Every time you do, you improve the way we tell this story.

In the section ahead, you'll learn why this company exists, how it started, who we serve, and how we do what we do.

1. Tell How Your Business Started

Then go right into your company's founding story. Early in your business's development you probably justified starting your business to everyone who would listen. What did you tell them? People love stories, in general, and anyone who's joining your business is particularly motivated to hear yours. Yet although these stories come up a lot in entrepreneur groups, they're rarely shared with employees. There are a lot of ways to add color to that story and establish an emotional bond with your new teammates. Here are just a few:

- What skill did you have that made you uniquely positioned to launch your business?

- If there was something you wanted to improve on in the place you worked before, what was it?

- What experiences did you have along the way that led to an aha moment and inspired what you're doing now?

Remember that scene where Jerry Maguire wrote a late-night manifesto and stormed out of his office to start his own business? Although your story may not be as dramatic, you probably have your own magic Maguire moment. Tell why and when you started the company, and what you did before the business that led you to start it. Put in everything you have reason to feel proud of.

Do you have:

- An aha moment from your last job?

- Something about a former boss that inspired you?

- A good story about your first customer that made you think you could turn this thing into a business?

- Any emotional case studies or testimonials about how you rescued some client early on?

- An email from the first person you helped who encouraged you to turn what you do into a business?

- Great early reviews following your grand opening?

Artifacts: Just as museums pique your interest by teaching about history through physical items, those you collect over time in your business are filled with stories to share with your new team members. For example, a barbershop might display a picture of its first haircut. Do you have artifacts you can show off? In our first year at Trainual, we had everyone sign a basketball. That ball's still in our office.

Do you have:

- The first T-shirt or business card you ever had printed?

- A screenshot of your first website?

- Your first client presentations?

- The first dollar you collected?

- An image of the first check you cashed for your business?

- The ribbon that was cut during your building's opening?

- Autographs by celebrity customers?

- A bottle of champagne from your first holiday party?

Journal: You're writing your history every day. If you're just getting started in your business (and you're still reading this book because you want to have a playbook when your business is ready for one), think about keeping notes and artifacts, and capturing your history as it happens. At Trainual, we're constantly collecting additions to our playbook. For example, as I'm writing this, our leadership team just wrapped a weekend trip to New England. I've packed pictures from the Boston Duck Tour and souvenirs from our visit to Fenway Park to add to our playbook when we get back.

More story ideas:

- Who were your first employees?

- Did any family members work there for free?

- Do any of the original team members still work for you?

- How did you or the founder decide on the company's name?

- If that name changed over time, is there a story worth telling about why?

- Has your logo evolved? If so, show the before-and-afters.

- Did your office start in your garage and then expand to multiple pins on the map?

- Coca-Cola's original recipe included cocaine! Has your recipe also changed with the times?

- Does your business's story include something truly outrageous? For example, Trainual's first employee, Chelsey Krisay, grew up in a family business. In an historic flood, the building that houses Krisay's Appliance & Bedding literally floated down the street—*landing on a new foundation,* where it still sits today. The story made it into Ripley's Believe It or Not! A story like that is hard to match, but your business probably has its own unforgettable details that could interest your new team members.

The stories paint the picture of what the company was like in its early years and highlight the progress you've made. They go a long way towards helping your new team members feel as though they're part of that progress.

2. Share Your Vision and Mission

You may have heard vision and mission defined in multiple ways. I follow the simple definition given to me by Clate Mask, the CEO of Keap and one of my mentors: a vision is something on the horizon that you never stop pursuing, while a mission is something concrete that you can achieve, like a single NASA lunar mission. (NASA's vision is vast: "We reach for new heights and reveal the unknown for the benefit of humankind.")

Your **vision** is where you expect your company is headed—an imagined end state. It's tied to your passion for the business, who you want to serve, and what kind of impact you want to make on the world. For example, back when only the biggest companies had computers, Microsoft's vision was "a computer on every desk." Trainual's vision is a playbook for every small business (that's ready for one).

Your vision might be to have an emotional impact on someone's life—to cure a disease or improve your community. No matter what, it should be something that's important to you and that will motivate yourself and your team to pursue it. Craft a simple statement of where you're headed and include it in the playbook. Don't concern yourself with making it perfect; it can and probably should evolve.

Related to vision, a **mission** is more tangible and measurable. It's what you're in business to do for people. A mission also tends to have a shorter-term perspective than the vision to help each person see their day-to-day contribution towards it. Like Elon Musk's plan to be on Mars by 2026, missions are far enough in the future that they feel like a challenge but not so far that your team can't see themselves accomplishing them. (His *vision* is to make humans into a multiplanetary species.)

Every working person is on a career path, and most people are unlikely to remain within one business for their entire career. A multiyear mission could attract people who so believe in it that they want to remain long enough to see it completed. Reid Hoffman, the co-founder of LinkedIn, refers to this possibility as a "tour of duty"—a term borrowed from the military, meaning something that people can sign up for and envision themselves seeing through.

Some people just start a business because they want to make money. But if you've started yours because you have a passion for what you're doing and the people you're doing it for, that passion will be baked into both the mission and the vision. For example, maybe someone's passion—and vision— is to cure a particular disease, and they've started a nonprofit with the mission of treating one million people, or launching some groundbreaking technology.

Trainual's current mission and focus is to reach 25,000—roughly 1 percent of—US-based small businesses by the end of 2022. It's a milestone we can achieve and rally our team around, but it's nowhere near the end state of our vision. When we make that milestone, we'll follow it up with another one.

Your vision and mission may live on your website and external marketing materials because they convey how you want to be known to the world—so it should also be how you want to be known within the company as people get started there.

3. Share Your Core Values

Next into the playbook should go your values. They're the traits and principles that you and your team members share. Establish them early *before* you document your processes. Documented core values make employees confident about taking action. Even before you have specific responses for every scenario you can anticipate, having core values in place will help guide your team's decisions in the right general direction.

For example, when COVID hit, it severely impacted a number of our small-business customers to the point that they could not pay their bills. Not only did we extend free access to our service, but we worked for free to help those customers use the downtime to build their playbooks. The cool part is, I wasn't even the one to suggest this. Our team has been built with helpfulness ingrained into our DNA, so when everything happened, the prevailing thought was, "How can we help?" That's the power of core values. Our team's helping attitude ties directly into one of ours (see "Carry the groceries" below).

Core values are different in every company, so avoid words like "hardworking," "smart," and "loyal"—those should apply to any- and everyone. Find what makes your culture unique and special. If you haven't identified your values yet, doing so should be your next step.

This exercise will help you find them: first think of someone you hired (or worked with at a previous company) who didn't work out for some reason. Maybe they failed the customers, clashed with the culture, didn't take the job seriously, or generally caused you to lose sleep. On a sheet of paper, list every one of that person's disappointing traits. These are your anti-values.

Now flip them into a positive: for instance, if it bothered you that they always showed up late, promptness might be one of your values. If you never felt as though you could count on them, maybe you value dependability.

Then think of an employee who represents the epitome of your culture. This is the person you wish you could clone a hundred times to take on every role in your business. Now list this person's attributes.

Boil down the two lists until you've identified five to eight values. To keep them from sounding like a motivational poster, turn each value into a memorable statement that your team can connect with.

How Trainual's Values Emerged

What might also help you come up with your values is walking through our company's process for coming up with ours.

When we did the exercise I just described, the first cluster of attributes we listed were "going above and beyond" and "being unexpectedly helpful." Brainstorming with them reminded me of when I was fourteen, bagging groceries at a local market. My job didn't include carrying them out, but I would do it anyway for people who seemed to need the help, whether because they were trying to wrangle kids or walking with a cane. I was being unexpectedly helpful, so **"Carry the groceries"** is our shorthand for encouraging our team to be unexpectedly helpful, too.

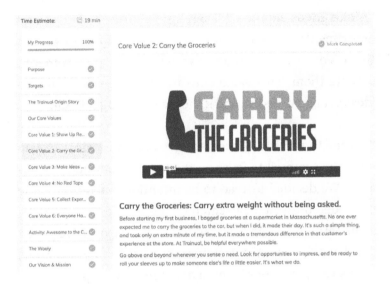

Time Estimate: 19 min

My Progress 100%

Core Value 2: Carry the Groceries ✓ Mark Completed

Purpose ✓
Targets ✓
The Trainual Origin Story ✓
Our Core Values ✓
Core Value 1: Show Up Re... ✓
Core Value 2: Carry the Gr... ✓
Core Value 3: Make Ideas ... ✓
Core Value 4: No Red Tape ✓
Core Value 5: Collect Exper... ✓
Core Value 6: Everyone Ha... ✓
Activity: Awesome to the C... ✓
The Wooly ✓
Our Vision & Mission ✓

Carry the Groceries: Carry extra weight without being asked.

Before starting my first business, I bagged groceries at a supermarket in Massachusetts. No one ever expected me to carry the groceries to the car, but when I did, it made their day. It's such a simple thing, and took only an extra minute of my time, but it made a tremendous difference in that customer's experience at the store. At Trainual, be helpful everywhere possible.

Go above and beyond whenever you sense a need. Look for opportunities to impress, and be ready to roll your sleeves up to make someone else's life a little easier. It's what we do.

Our five other values are "Everyone has a key," "Make ideas happen," "No red tape," "Collect experiences," and "Show up ready."

"Everyone has a key" is all about ownership and autonomy. From the beginning of the business, we made the decision that team members could come and go as they pleased and work remotely, as long as they got results. We did that to encourage everyone to act like an owner and make decisions without much intervention. We also take the value literally: our office has a key-card system that anyone can access 24/7.

"Make ideas happen." There's no shortage of ideas and experimentation in the early days of a startup. But I've seen that it's one thing to come up with the ideas and another to execute them. This value aims to encourage the latter, so ideas get listed, tested, and if they work, brought to life.

"No red tape." In any business, as you create processes, you might be tempted to layer on the bureaucracy and compliance. We decided instead to be intentional about avoiding unneeded bureaucracy—empowering people to make decisions without having to fill out forms and reports and to just do what's right for the customer. By establishing this value, we also empower our team to hold the mirror up to us if we start to introduce red tape.

"Collect experiences" is about work–life balance. This value is there to remind us that even though we all work for the company, we also have lives outside of it. Our team members have diverse backgrounds and hobbies. Those experiences enable us all to bring something rich and unique to work.

"Show up ready" came out of our consulting roots. Just as it sounds, the value is all about showing up organized and ready to perform for meetings, both internal and external. That includes doing research, making an agenda, staying efficient, and appearing polished and professional at all times.

The Best Way to Communicate Values to Your Team

Once you come up with your core values, help them sink in for your team by reinforcing and giving an example of each one. For example, we decided to reinforce "Collect experiences" by creating a $500 annual benefit for every employee to pay for any new and enriching experience they want to have outside of work. It might be signing up for a race or a class, taking guitar lessons, traveling somewhere new to them, or trying some exotic cuisine. All employees have to do in exchange is to share a photo or story to commemorate the experience. That, in turn, helps new hires understand the value.

For example, one of our employees decided to participate in his first triathlon, so he used his benefit money to sign up and buy a used bike to ride in it. He shared photos of his training and then crossing the finish line. It inspired and excited the company to be able to celebrate that achievement and support his transformation.

For each value, we had a designer create a graphic, and I recorded a quick video telling the story of the value in no more than sixty seconds. Then we added some text and photos for the examples, like the triathlon story. The format you choose is, of course, up to you, as long as you stay away from just presenting text, which would be too boring to inspire anyone.

To help your team better visualize the value, you could also put each one on a coffee cup, wall decal, or T-shirt. Or put it on an award, as we do. Every month, we hand out an award to the person who best exemplified one of the values that month. In the playbook, we have photos of every past winner.

4. Communicate Your Brand

If you're a marketing firm or consumer products company, you probably give more attention to your brand than if you're, say, a manufacturer or parts supplier, but everyone has a brand. This part of your playbook is your chance to convey the look and feel of your business to your new team members. It's your business's personality, voice, and tone—whether professional and structured, quirky and casual, or something else entirely.

Your brand includes several components, like your logo, your website design, maybe a color scheme, and the imagery you tend to use. It might show up on your water bottles, T-shirts, hats, or any other swag you order for your team members and customers. In addition to handing out the swag to new hires, you could put photos of it in the playbook. My company embraced the sports playbook analogy, so we give all new hires a basketball jersey with our logo on the front and their name and employee numbers on the back.

You might want to go a step further by adding a detailed brand guide to your playbook to include variations on your logo, registered trademarks, slogans, and the thirty-second elevator pitch on your brand. That way, if a new employee bumps into a friend who asks what their new company is like, they've got a built-in, brand-aligned way to talk about it.

One thing to keep in mind about your brand is that its introduction in the profile should be high-level enough to apply to everyone. More detailed information, like for a brand manager, will go in the process section for that role.

5. Introduce Your Market/Industry, Customers, and Competitors

When people search for your company online, in what category do they find you? How are you represented in the marketplace? To orient new hires to the space your business belongs in, start this part of the playbook by touching on your category or industry (unless it's too obvious for words).

Next describe the customer you most want to attract and serve. Some companies introduce this ideal customer as a persona—a made-up person with a name and attributes, like their family situation.

Finally, list your most successful competitors for the same customers and the features that give you the edge over them. Your team should be prepared to respond in case your potential customers ask.

6. Introduce Your Products and Services

Just as most restaurants have a menu to make it obvious what dishes they sell, use this part of the playbook to list your company's menu of products or services and their approximate prices. By listing them, you're not (necessarily) asking every employee to become a sales rep for your company, but to have a basic understanding of what you deliver to your customer.

And if you have too many products to expect your non-sales reps to learn, your people should at least be able to speak about broad product lines. You never know when someone behind the scenes might have the opportunity to promote what you do—even in casual conversations with friends.

7. Introduce Company-wide Software

Provide a basic intro to only the software tools that apply to everyone, like your email and calendar programs, and chat app, if you use them. New hires will be expected to use these programs early on. Each department and role is likely to use other platforms that apply specifically to their work, but those don't belong in the Profile section.

Also limit included logins or passwords to the ones for the platforms that everyone needs access to, like a vendor portal. Of course you wouldn't include people's private individual logins to various software programs.

8. Include a Glossary

Every industry and business has its own jargon—acronyms and other terms that someone coming into the business off the street might not have been exposed to. It's helpful to spell those out because for the people who've worked there a while, those terms quickly became so second-nature that they probably don't remember that they didn't always know them. Nor will they remember to define them for the newcomers. The glossary will go a long way towards aiding communication during their first weeks at your company.

9. Introduce How Your Business Works

The final piece of the profile is a start-to-finish look at what actually goes on in your company so that each employee understands their place in the big picture.

I learned the importance of sharing that understanding when I ran my video company. At first, my camera operators would show up, turn on the camera, and hit record. Because they didn't know what happened before and after the shooting in the business cycle, I got a lot of refund requests. Customers were unhappy because the operator would miss important details like a particular figure skater's move that a judge had to study. It quickly became obvious that the operators needed more context to do a good job.

One way to begin to share that big-picture view is to think about how a dollar tends to flow through the business. You can include an illustration of that process in your playbook if a visual makes sense for your business. I used this diagram for my video business to give a quick overview to the hundreds of camera operators we hired.

Along with a quick explanation, the macro view helped them understand at a glance how their work fit within the context of the whole company and encouraged them to innovate beyond their role.

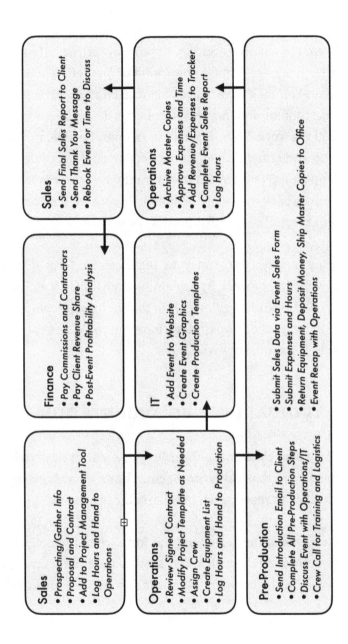

Sales
- Prospecting/Gather Info
- Proposal and Contract
- Add to Project Management Tool
- Log Hours and Hand to Operations

Operations
- Review Signed Contract
- Modify Project Template as Needed
- Assign Crew
- Create Equipment List
- Log Hours and Hand to Production

Pre-Production
- Send Introduction Email to Client
- Complete All Pre-Production Steps
- Discuss Event with Operations/IT
- Crew Call for Training and Logistics

Finance
- Pay Commissions and Contractors
- Pay Client Revenue Share
- Post-Event Profitability Analysis

IT
- Add Event to Website
- Create Event Graphics
- Create Production Templates

- Submit Sales Data via Event Sales Form
- Submit Expenses and Hours
- Return Equipment, Deposit Money, Ship Master Copies to Office
- Event Recap with Operations

Sales
- Send Final Sales Report to Client
- Send Thank You Message
- Rebook Event or Time to Discuss

Operations
- Archive Master Copies
- Approve Expenses and Time
- Add Revenue/Expenses to Tracker
- Complete Event Sales Report
- Log Hours

To begin the chain of events, you probably attract attention for your business through some kind of marketing effort or referral. You may have a sales team to convert those leads into customers, and maybe you collect a deposit before you kick off the work. Then, if you have an operations team, they take the order and deliver the product or service. A customer-support rep is there to make sure the customer is happy and comes back with more business. Finally, the accountant or bookkeeper bills for that product or service.

Imagine how much better your team can perform if they know your full process. By explaining each link in the chain, you provide the macro view of how they fit into the company. That context encourages innovations that could serve others outside of their narrow role.

ONBOARDING VS. ORIENTATION

You may hear the terms onboarding, orientation, and training used interchangeably throughout the process of getting a new hire up to speed, so let me clarify those here.

Onboarding is the period of time from when the new hire accepts an offer through when they're fully productive in their role in the company. The initial administrative steps could involve signing a formal offer, adding the employee to payroll, and other legally required filings.

Orientation is the process we've described above, where you introduce the person to your company's profile.

Training kicks off after the general orientation, as the new hire begins to ramp up in their role, which we'll cover later in the "Process" element.

GETTING INTO THE (COMFORT) ZONE

Before your playbook dives into the weeds on who's in your company, what rules govern it, and how your business does what it does, there's so much that new hires need to know to feel comfortable in their new work setting. That's the story of your business. Start there, and you'll get all your team members aligned.

By the time I left my college's summer orientation, I felt only excited about my upcoming new adventure. When I returned for my first day of class, I was proud of my new college and ready to work hard. That's also what a great business profile does. It helps orient new hires, gives them the big picture, and makes them feel part of the team.

Another big part of understanding a culture and feeling comfortable inside the business for a new hire is getting to know the people they'll be working with. The next chapter will show you how to craft that second element in your playbook.

PROFILE TOPICS CHECKLIST

☐ Video Greeting

☐ Company History

☐ Founding Story

☐ Artifacts

☐ Vision

☐ Mission

☐ Core Values

☐ Brand Standards

☐ Company Messaging

☐ Market/Industry

☐ Customers

☐ Competitors

☐ Products and Services

☐ Software Tools

☐ Industry Glossary

☐ How Your Business Works

☐ Basic Company Info:

☐ Company Address(s)

☐ Company Phone Number(s)

☐ Social Media Accounts

☐ Hours of Operation

☐ Where to Park

☐ Office Map

☐ Approved Vendor List

4

YOUR PEOPLE: MAKING THE MAP FOR WHO'S WHO AND WHAT THEY DO

Five years into my video-production company, I still didn't know too much about how business works in the "real world." I remember picking up a copy of *Videomaker*, an industry magazine, and seeing a full-page ad for a conference where I could get my hands on the latest camera gear and meet other people that were doing what I was doing. As a nineteen-year-old business newbie, that sounded like Disneyland. I booked the trip to Jacksonville, Florida.

It felt like my first real investment in the business. It was definitely my first business conference. Walking in, I suppose I

expected a welcome like the one I got in my college orientation. But this experience was nothing like that. I stood
alone in the crowded registration line feeling like a stranger
at someone else's family reunion. And twenty minutes later,
when I reached the front of the line, it turned out that I
should have been checking in at a different table around the
corner.

The rest of the week, I sat disconnected in the last row of
these big lecture halls. Without having attended year after
year, I had no good way to break into what felt like a big
clique. There were no meet-and-greets, no welcomes, and
no chance I'd be returning the next year.

Years later, I went to a different conference, and the experience was dramatically different.

Maybe you've seen one of the famous TED Talks, like Simon
Sinek telling you to "start with why" or Brené Brown recom-
mending that you let yourself be vulnerable. When TED
hit my radar, I decided to give the whole conference thing
another go and ended up with a friend at TEDActive near
Palm Springs, California.

From the moment I signed up, I immediately began to get
emails that made me feel like part of an exclusive club.
They sent a series of books in advance, with notes about

how the themes would relate to our event. Weeks before I ever got on the plane, I downloaded a directory app, where I could browse the other attendees, sort by industry or location, and message back and forth in real time to build relationships.

When it was time to get into *this* registration line, before I could summon that old feeling of dread, the guy behind me tapped me on the shoulder and said, "Hey, Chris! Great to see you in real life!" The experience kept repeating itself. I was instantly part of a community instead of needing to fend for myself. It felt great. The conference developers had created that level of intimacy despite having twice the attendees of the video show, and I bet you can guess which group of attendees I keep in touch with to this day.

GET PEOPLE ACQUAINTED

In the same way that TED brought me into the fold, you want new hires to quickly feel as though they belong, not like a stranger for their first three months. That's the difference that knowing people can make, and it's what this section of the playbook is about: introducing everyone, sharing what they do at work and in their spare time so there are plenty of conversation starters, mentioning how their roles overlap, and reducing potential awkwardness.

Sure, you gave newcomers a warm welcome in the profile section, but when you introduce the other players, it's as if the welcome is also coming from them. You can bet that before they even start, your new employees are googling and social-media-stalking their future teammates, trying to get a sense of the people and the culture. So, this proactive introduction can save them time and fill in some gaps.

CREATE A BROWSABLE PEOPLE DIRECTORY

You might remember visiting a shopping mall and immediately seeking out that giant, backlit directory of stores. You probably found the store you were looking for by its category (computers, shoes, jewelry) in a long list, then looked for the store's code on the floor plan next to the list. To call your attention to new stores, some malls highlight them—"COMING THIS FALL"—on the directory.

That's the same idea as the people directory for your company: It should be an easy-to-browse internal list of all the people who make up your organization. Group them by team, location, role, store, and/or whatever makes sense for your business. At the very least, along with the person's name, each listing should include their photo and job title and anything else it would be useful to see at a glance.

Like the highlighted new stores in a mall, your directory should indicate when team members are newly added, so everyone can anticipate their arrival and maybe make the extra effort to get to know them early in their employment.

The directory doesn't need to be complicated, but it does need to be centralized, easy to navigate, and up to date. When I was consulting, I used to dig around on client websites and scour their "team" pages, only to find that too often, those public pages were filled with employees who no longer worked at the business. The most common excuse? One of those past employees was the one who managed the website.

Being out of date doesn't work for a website, and it definitely doesn't work for a playbook. Not only does it give new employees a false sense of who works there, but it also looks shabby and as if the people who work there don't really matter. By contrast, a directory that is up to date and highlights everyone shows employees that they're valued.

Here is an example of a simple people directory inside Trainual:

PRESENT AN ORG CHART

A browsable directory is just one way to help people visualize your entire team. Another popular view is the organizational

chart. Even in the most progressive Silicon Valley startups that swear by their horizontal, hierarchy-free structure, the reality is most employees still report to someone else. They have someone to go to for direction, career coaching, and help with daily decisions. It's still typical for a company's structure to grow with the company, and good old-fashioned org charts aren't going anywhere.

Like a blueprint for a house, an org chart is a simple and digestible way to illustrate the company's structure—who reports to each manager, the relative size of departments, and even relationships between satellite offices and headquarters.

You can also use the org chart as a tool to brainstorm and project where you expect the business to be in the future. I recommend producing the org chart you have today and the one you expect to have twelve months from now: your "Future Org Chart." I realize you don't know the names of people in jobs you don't have yet, but the exercise of envisioning those gaps and how they might be filled will get you thinking about which areas you expect to grow and where you might need senior leaders versus team members. The org chart becomes your best predictor of where you'll need to invest in more people.

You might also put your existing team members inside all the present and future boxes for the roles they have today. In small businesses, individuals wear a lot of hats, and the Future Org Chart exercise helps you illustrate exactly how many hats each person is wearing. For example, let's say you start with a single marketing employee (let's call her Becky, after ours). Though she's only one person, she may currently be managing your PR, social media, and newsletter. With another year's worth of growth, you might expect to hire full-time roles for a PR manager, social media manager, and a content writer. For now, put Becky's name in all three boxes to help yourself and your team visualize the number and type of people you'll need to bring in as the business grows.

Although Trainual began with only five of us, we sketched out a fifty-person org chart in our early days. Three years later, we surpassed that number of employees, but we maintain a rolling twelve-month Future Org Chart inside our playbook to give everyone a sense of where we're going.

One of the biggest challenges any new business goes through is converting to a more complicated structure. When you're adding in that next layer to your org chart, it's another signal that you need a playbook.

How to Build It

If somehow you've made it this far in your career without seeing an org chart, I can tell you its mechanics are pretty simple—essentially, boxes and lines. Just place each person's name, title, and maybe a short description inside a box (round the corners if you're fancy). Then, add lines showing how each person connects with—manages, reports to, or is at the same level as—other entries. If you're graphically inclined, feel free to add avatar photos, but those are covered in your directory. Again, the org chart's main purpose is showing relationships between roles more than showcasing the people themselves.

Here's an example for a small team of ten people:

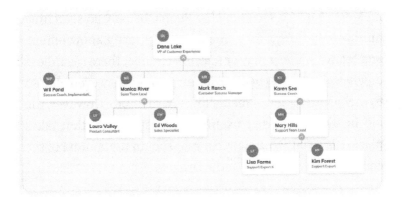

BUILD THE BIOS

Just as your business has a profile, every person who works in your business has a profile or bio that helps other people get to know them. This biographical intro is not meant to replace having people meet each other in person. You're not including it to remove the personal side of their relationships.

Instead, think of the bio as a way to preview and supplement the in-person experience. They help to satisfy people's initial curiosity about each other. If that bio brings up commonalities, like maybe they went to the same school, it makes their in-person meeting that much warmer.

You may be thinking, "But isn't that what Facebook, LinkedIn, and Instagram are for?" Actually, no. The bio is not meant to replace social media. People usually go searching on those platforms for someone they already know offline, and team members may or may not connect there regardless of what's in the playbook. Your employees may even choose to include their social media links in their bio. However, the bio in the playbook is useful *before* any interaction takes place. It's an entry point and a snapshot in the context of the company they'll work together in.

(Bios can also be helpful for vendors, investors, or anyone else who sees the benefit of learning about your team but may not be likely to interact with them on social media.)

DIY Bios: Ask each new hire to write their own, and let them know they can update it any time they want. As soon as they accept the job offer, invite them to browse the team's bios to get a head start on writing their own—typically 250 words or less. We ask employees to come up with theirs on their first day.

Your team members aren't likely to include anything inappropriate, but if you're at all concerned, before the bios are published, you could run them by each person's direct report. (But if you're really that concerned on their first day, maybe think about tightening up your interview process to find people you can trust!)

Bio Element Options

At the very least, the digital introduction includes a brief narrative of each person: who they are, what their role is in the company, and why you'd go to them. But it can contain so much more.

You might suggest that employees include hobbies and other interests. For the same reason, people often include things like their family structure, where they grew up, maybe their favorite sports team, or what they love about their work specialty. In an increasingly remote world, sharing parts of what makes them unique helps employees to forge important connections.

On a more practical note, you might also ask that employees add a brief purpose statement about why their role exists in the company. For example, maybe they were hired to make sure the customers are happy, to keep the software running without bugs, or to maintain the brand standards.

And, if the company has multiple locations or if people work primarily remotely, they might want to include their time zone and general working hours. It's also helpful to include contact info, user names on other communications tools, and social media profiles. If you use any personality assessments or strengths assessments, people could also share their results here as a clue for how to best work with them.

Last, I recommend that you add when each person joined the team because it helps new people understand seniority and (sometimes) influence. They want to be able to easily distinguish between someone who's worked at the company for ten years and held seven roles versus someone who showed up only a month before.

LIST ROLES AND RESPONSIBILITIES

The most fundamental connection between the people in your business and the business itself isn't their title, their interests, their contact info, or their direct reports. It's what they actually *do*—their responsibilities. These come in many forms. From vague bullet points in a job description to complicated tasks that only the employee is aware that they're doing, responsibilities are the fabric of the business, and not having them spelled out is the fastest way for a company to create chaos.

When a company is growing and changing as much as yours probably is, responsibilities are never stagnant. People are taking on new ones and maybe handing off old ones. You need to keep them up-to-date and organized, which is an ideal way to round out the people element of the playbook.

The number one problem that comes up in small businesses is a misalignment of roles and responsibilities. When someone doesn't know what's expected of them or when they were hired to do a job that's the opposite of what they're doing today, they're not likely to stay for long. A person's career path should never feel murky.

If you remember anything from this book, it should be the need to create clearly outlined roles and responsibilities.

Responsibilities just seem to pour onto each person's plate. Whether they show up regularly or sporadically, these might be tasks that the employee is not even conscious of doing. A typical place for responsibilities to emerge is through the job description that goes in a job posting—often the earliest indication that you're starting to formalize responsibilities.

Both for your employee's sake and for yours, keep responsibilities from quietly shifting by keeping them deliberate, formal, and updated in the bio as they (intentionally) change. It's one of the biggest-impact things you can do because it shows everyone that you're putting attention into what's on their plate, even if only one person is doing a thing.

Like the bio, responsibilities are best outlined by the employee. Here's an exercise to harvest all the responsibilities of every person in your business. By the end of that activity, you'll have collected the source material for standard operating procedures that you might decide to document in depth later on. Here are five suggestions to help each team member come up with a comprehensive list:

Brainstorm one typical day: At least every year, if not every quarter or two, ask each established employee—from the intern to the CEO—to brainstorm everything they're doing now. (Of course, you won't ask new hires to do this until they get up to speed on their job.) Ask your employees to start with a typical day from starting to quitting time. They should include even the trivial-sounding things, like disarming the alarm system when they arrive, combing the mail for invoices and checks, and checking and responding to email.

Brainstorm by activity period: Then ask them to think of certain days of the week—maybe there's a report they run every Monday, a weekly meeting they facilitate, or a recurring webinar they host. Then they should think about the month (like paying monthly sales tax), the quarter (like setting quarterly goals), and the year (like performance reviews).

Survey your outbox: Another useful hack is having each person go through the past two weeks of their outgoing messages (assuming you use email in your business). That's the email you've actually engaged with—messages you've forwarded and requests you've made and replied to—and it's a clue to how you've spent your time. Why two weeks? That tends to be a typical business cycle, but feel free to adjust the timeline to fit yours.

Check the calendar: Also ask people to go through up to a month's worth of appointments, meetings, projects, and deadlines in their calendars. With such a visual medium, it's easier to look at a longer period than if you're sorting through email.

Browse apps: And if your company uses a live chat system, a task-management or project-management tool, a CRM, or any other industry application that you track your work in, that's yet another place to find pieces of the responsibilities puzzle.

By the end of the search, every team member should have come up with an exhaustive list of the things they do in the company. That might add up to thousands of micro responsibilities across your team that might not require much documentation detail but should have a place in the playbook.

That way, even if the watercooler is getting empty, you know which person in the office should take the lead on reordering.

And even if you don't end up fully documenting your policies and processes, you'll find it enlightening to create this master responsibilities list. It will help trigger discussion when you meet one-on-one with your team members. You can tell at a glance if they're doing too much, if they're not doing something you thought they were responsible for, or if something fell through the cracks.

Or maybe you hired a contractor to take on one of their tasks, but they're having to spend so much time babysitting that contractor that it's counterproductive. The process of working with a responsibilities list uncovers those types of inefficiencies.

WHAT REALLY MATTERS

People are the most important part of your business. Even though every company's profile is unique, it can be similar in some ways to that of another business. But it's the people who really make the difference. They're who make your business what—and *who*—it is. It pays to invest in helping everyone feel welcome and get acquainted and in keeping their responsibilities aligned with them.

When you think about the dramatic difference between my two conference experiences, I know there's no question about which experience you want for your new employees. By building a directory, an org chart, friendly bios, and detailed roles and responsibilities, you're creating a sense of belonging for your new team members and setting them up for success.

Even if they feel welcomed to the team, however, most employees loathe the dreaded company handbook. It's often seen as a necessary evil, but it doesn't have to be that way. In the next chapter, you'll find out how to have and share essential policies without letting them destroy the culture of your business.

PEOPLE TOPICS CHECKLIST

☐ People Directory

☐ Employee Names

☐ Employee Titles

☐ Department/Team Structure

☐ Current Org Chart

☐ Future Org Chart

☐ Employee Career Background

☐ Employee Bios

☐ Company Start Date

☐ Social Media Profiles

☐ Employee Images/Videos

☐ Time Zone

☐ General Working Hours

☐ Strengths Assessment Results

☐ Roles

☐ Responsibilities—Brainstorm by:

    ☐ Daily

    ☐ Weekly

    ☐ Biweekly

☐ Monthly

☐ Quarterly

☐ Annually

☐ Email Outbox

☐ Calendar

☐ Project Management System

☐ Chat Software (and others!)

5

YOUR POLICIES: WRITING THE RULES OF PLAY

Towards the end of Trainual's first year in business, I was at a pool on vacation with my family when I got a frightening call. With a shaky voice, the wife of our lead developer told me that he had been rushed to the ER and then into surgery because of a life-threatening medical emergency.

Their family went through an incredibly trying time, including his induced coma and forty days in an out-of-state intensive-care unit. During all of this, his wife would call me to ask about issues I had never thought of, like what was our short-term disability policy? (Our *what*?) What kind of documentation did we need from the hospital and his doctor so he could continue getting paid? How long would he continue to receive benefits? Would his job be there for him when he returned?

Out of nowhere, my five-person company was thrust into a difficult situation and hit with the kind of questions that I thought only big, mature companies had to deal with.

But my inability to foresee every potential issue wasn't the only reason I didn't have all the policies in place that I should have. I've never liked red tape (see the Core Values section in Chapter 3). To keep things simple in my businesses, both for my sake and for my employees, I've always tried to avoid it. But my team member's emergency taught us all that sometimes simplicity doesn't work. When people going through traumatic situations need real answers, you need black-and-white guidelines to support them.

If you too have resisted policies because you thought you could get away with it, you really can't. Everyone on your team will be better off if you take the time to proactively establish policies that support them *before* an urgent situation forces you to make things up on the fly. You can't predict how the employee issues will show up, only that they will. So many legitimate emergencies can happen to interfere with an employee's ability to work, and you need to be ready to respond when it happens.

THE THREE TYPES
OF POLICIES YOU NEED

You might be glad to know that the Policy section in your playbook doesn't have to be boring, bureaucratic, or complicated. But it does need to communicate to your team members three main types of policy information: what legal requirements your business must comply with, what benefits are available to them, and how they're expected to behave.

The policies section of your playbook is a contemporary version of an employee handbook. If you already have a handbook, review it through the lens of this chapter for its suitability to drop in. It's best if you can do it through software, so it's customizable, searchable, and easier to update.

Let's look at the details, one at a time:

1. The Legal Stuff

You need to know what you're legally obligated to do as a business and what you must share with your employees about what the law won't tolerate, like harassment or using illicit drugs. If you don't, you could face needless disruption, like getting in trouble with your government or having a former employee sue you. That's why you should start your policies section with your legal requirements.

In my video business, I hired an HR consultant to make sure we were abiding by all applicable laws. I couldn't begin to sift through them all by myself. I recommend that you do the same, or work with an employment lawyer. If you work with a professional employer organization (PEO) for your HR and payroll, they're likely to be able to provide guidance in this area as well. Here, I'll start you off with some basic things you can consider before you meet with them.

Include laws that apply to your company based on its type, starting with size. More laws will affect your business as it grows. And they change all the time, so don't hold me to this example: as I write this chapter, a US company with a minimum of fifteen employees is bound by antidiscrimination laws, and with a minimum of fifty employees, by FMLA (Family and Medical Leave Act) policies. You might easily grow beyond one of those thresholds and naively infringe on a law you weren't aware of.

Also look for laws that apply to your business based on where it's located, like a minimum wage you must comply with, taxes you must file and pay, or posters you must display.

There are also legal implications for the industry you're in. For example, manufacturing has safety protocols, and hospitality has food-handling laws.

You might be legally required to keep a record that you've not only stated the policies to your employees but that they've read and formally acknowledged them. Our software records these events with time and date stamps, but you can do it any way you want as long as you're consistent about it.

2. Benefits

Devote the next part of the policies section in the playbook to a comprehensive guide to the unique mix of benefits you offer, and when, how, and maybe which employees qualify for them. For example, maybe certain benefits apply based on an employee's tenure with the company. And, depending again on the size of your company, some benefits may be legally required, like paying a certain portion of full-time employees' health insurance premiums.

When I was hiring my high school friends to work in my video business, the idea of benefits wasn't even on my radar. If someone had asked me about the benefits of working for me, I would've said, "Getting to make seven dollars an hour hanging out with your friends." I might've added that the absence of actual benefits and my limited overhead were a competitive advantage. But without benefits, as the company grew, I couldn't attract the higher-level employees we needed to deal with the increasing complexity of the business.

By the time I founded Trainual, I knew I needed to both offer and communicate attractive benefits. Each year our benefits got richer, and every time, those upgrades made it into the playbook, so each new employee would be aware of them. Also, with benefits centralized in the playbook, everyone also knows exactly where to look when they have questions.

Documenting some benefits might be as simple as pasting in your insurance carrier's premiums, deductibles, and contact info, while others could require more detailed explanation, supplemented with videos that share more about how each works.

For instance, our playbook includes a stock-options section that teaches the basics of vesting and exercising options and calculating their value. I included a video with additional commentary because this topic raised a lot of questions among our employees.

(By the way, while you're documenting benefits, there's no better time to make sure they're appropriate for your company's culture and maturity level.)

3. Cultural Norms

Every policy that isn't governed by a law or that doesn't reflect a benefit falls into the bucket of cultural norms. These policies include the kind of behavior that's not legally mandated. It's also the policy area that varies the most by company type and company. For example, I don't mean to stereotype, but consider a typical boutique development shop versus a typical Fortune 500 firm. Those two images are laden with dozens of different cultural norms. To make sure your team is acting in alignment with your vision, you need to spell out your norms.

This includes dress code: can people wear slippers, shorts, and band T-shirts, or is "business casual" or formal attire required?

Norms also include behavior, for example:

- Can employees play music while they work?

- Is it okay to use the ping-pong table during the day?

- Do employees need to be at their desks for a set number of hours?

- Can people make personal calls on the job?

- Are they restricted in what they can say on social media?

- Can employees date each other?

- What's your remote-work policy?

- How much leave notice do employees need to give?

It's worth mentioning again that employees who resist your cultural norms might be in the wrong company. Setting your cultural norms—along with the mission and vision—is an authentic representation of the business you want to build and should help you attract the kind of people who'll align with and sign off on them. In fact, the most common reason new hires don't work out is that they unknowingly misalign with the company's unwritten cultural norms.

With all the remote work going on, clearly expressing cultural norms is more important than ever. It's a lot harder to pick up on them on a Zoom screen than when you can walk into the business, interact with people in person, and observe cultural norms in practice.

We have a cultural-norm policy that we developed early on in the video business when employees would text me at all hours. Often covering late-night events at different time zones from mine, they'd forget I had a different schedule. That experience turned into a set of communication policies about response turnaround by format: within twenty-four hours to an email, the end of the day to a Slack message, and a few hours to a voicemail, "But if you text me, I'll assume it's crazy urgent and get right back to you."

We established the same policies at Trainual with an emphasis on avoiding bothering people with unimportant questions during off-hours. Everyone appreciates that level of respect.

BE READY TO ADAPT

When you're building policies into the playbook, plan for what you can, while anticipating there will be things you can't anticipate. Stuff happens, like our developer's health emergency, and policies need to respond when it does. Of course, nothing could have been less predictable than the pandemic. In our business and most others, it affected legal, benefits, and cultural policies.

There was also some overlap, like the new law that applied to our benefits package: extending paid time off to employees who had been exposed to COVID-19.

So much also changed culturally, like how we communicated things to the team, such as when it was safe to come into the office and for how many people at a time. (We prioritized people who didn't have working space at home.) We took other proactive precautions, like putting up signage about safety, requiring masks to be worn, installing air purifiers, adding space between desks, and providing hand sanitizer and individually packaged foods. At the same time, we successfully navigated the business side so that we were able to retain every employee.

While all this was going on, we were combing through our playbook and updating it in real time to communicate the changes and roll them out to everyone. It made the experience go so much more smoothly than it could have.

NO ONE-SIZE-FITS-ALL
APPROACH: *CUSTOMIZE*

Choosing the policies that make sense for your business is only half the task ahead of you. The other half is figuring out how to roll them out to your team. Different policies will apply to different roles or geographic locations. For example, there's no point in training your call-center employees in the travel policies that only the sales reps care about.

To avoid drowning people in policies they don't need to be trained in, group categories of policies in your playbook so that each person can easily find what they need for their role and location. (In Chapter 7, you'll learn more about how to roll out your playbook.)

NO KNEE-JERK POLICIES

Wherever your business is located, I'll bet your local government has at least a few insane laws on the books. In Arizona, Trainual's home base, it's actually illegal for donkeys to sleep in bathtubs![2] That's a throwback to an incident that took place on a ranch in 1924: when a dam broke, a donkey that liked to nap in a discarded tub on the property got washed away and was tough to rescue. In their infinite wisdom, the townspeople demanded the law to prevent such a random event in the future.

Weird as it sounds, a similar thing happens in companies. In fact, I came close to making it happen in mine. In our second office, we finally had a kitchen, and employees started stocking the fridge. They especially liked bringing Cokes in glass

---

2 "Donkeys Cannot Sleep in Bathtubs," Stupid Laws, https://www.stupidlaws.com/donkeys-cannot-sleep-in-bathtubs/.

bottles. One day, when I swung open the refrigerator, a single bottle fell from the door, smashed, and made a mess. My knee-jerk reaction was a no-glass policy.

I had to stop and realize that a) it was my fault and b) it was unlikely to happen again. We'd had the kitchen for the previous nine months without breakage. So unless glass crashes started happening a lot, we didn't need a policy. In two more years of many more glass bottles in the fridge, nothing has broken. If I had overreacted by insisting on that policy, imagine how people would've rolled their eyes at my lapse in judgment. And, it would have directly conflicted with our core value of "No red tape."

NO FOREVER POLICIES

You've heard that rules are made to be broken, and that could not be truer when it comes to business. Make it a *policy* to regularly review your policies. To avoid overwhelming your team, throw away policies that no longer—or never did— make sense.

For example, when Trainual started, it was just one project amid a dozen other software and consulting projects that our team was juggling. So, every day, our team spent time logging their hours for the consulting work by task down to the billable minute. As Trainual picked up steam and replaced the consulting projects, I realized that everyone was still logging their minutes for more than six months since I had sent our last consulting invoice. When I got rid of the policy, the team breathed a sigh of relief. Over the course of a year, not having to track time saved us a lot of time: even with only five people, when we each stopped wasting twenty minutes per week in tracking time, we collectively regained more than ten days of productivity per year.

In most businesses, people are doing obsolete policy-based tasks that were established years ago because no one has questioned them since. To avoid this waste of time, regularly review your policies and ask your team to suggest ones to get rid of. At team meetings, celebrate these removals and maybe even reward the people who suggest them.

THE BOTTOM LINE

You've seen here that policies should never be about eye-roll-worthy layers of red tape. They need to be useful, fair, clear, and never overreactive. The policies you choose are an important way to start conversations, enhance your culture, and proactively invest in the experience of your team members.

The day that my developer's wife called me at the pool, it was instantly and abundantly clear that I hadn't put enough thought into the policies at our company. I was scrambling to come up with answers during the most stressful time in their lives. Although I never would have wished for something like that to happen, it caused us to put important work into our policies and playbook, and now we're much more prepared for the unexpected.[3]

In the next chapter, we'll get into the moment you've been waiting for: the standard operating procedures, best practices, and how-tos that make up a large part of your company's playbook. Dive in to learn how to present them most effectively.

POLICIES TOPICS CHECKLIST

There are dozens of potential policies that you may want to consider for your business. Some we've discussed above, and I've included additional options below to help you brainstorm as you outline your playbook.

---

3 In case you're wondering, the employee made a full recovery and returned to the company, where he remains.

Legal Policies

☐ At-will Employment

☐ Confidentiality Agreement

☐ Conflict of Interest

☐ Resignation/Termination Policy

☐ Drug and Alcohol Policy

☐ Employee Confidentiality

☐ Employee Privacy

☐ Equal Opportunity

☐ Ethics and Conduct Policies

☐ Noncompete Policy

☐ Nondiscrimination Policy

☐ Sexual Harassment Policy

☐ Weapons/Workplace Violence

☐ Laws Based on Company Size

☐ Laws Based on Company Location

Benefits

☐ Benefits Packages

☐ Bereavement Leave Policy

☐ Paid Time Off

☐ Sick Days

☐ Maternity and Paternity Leave

☐ Employee Compensation

☐ Employment Classifications

☐ Worker's Compensation

☐ Short-Term Disability

☐ Long-Term Disability

☐ Life Insurance

☐ 401(k)

☐ Stock Options

☐ Benefits Based on Tenure

Cultural Norms

☐ Pay Periods

☐ Holiday Schedule

☐ Flexible Work Hours

☐ BYOD (Bring Your Own Device)

☐ Code of Conduct

☐ Communication Policy

☐ Attendance Policy

☐ Credit Card Usage

- ☐ Diversity and Inclusion

- ☐ Dress Code

- ☐ Issuing Employee Complaints

- ☐ Employee Professional Development

- ☐ Tracking Expenses

- ☐ Meal and Break Periods

- ☐ Mobile Phone Policy

- ☐ Nonsmoking Policy

- ☐ Open-Door Policy

- ☐ Social Media Policy

- ☐ Remote Work Policy

- ☐ Recruitment Policy

- ☐ Technology Policy

- ☐ Company Travel Guidelines

☐ Workplace Health and Safety

☐ Noise Policy

☐ Leave Notice

☐ Employee Fraternization

6

YOUR PROCESSES: SHIFTING FROM "HOW YOU DO IT" TO "HOW *WE* DO IT"

You know those fast-food restaurants that run on an assembly line? They add the ingredients you choose as you walk past them on your way to paying and getting your food. They've got the concept of process so dialed in that everything moves along smoothly. Things just work. That should be every business owner's goal.

On my first visit to a new client, a commercial printing company, I was looking for that sort of assembly-line approach. But, as in most businesses, it was nowhere to be found. There was no sense of order or connection between departments (or even clear-cut departments to begin with).

There was also no consistent process for handling orders; I watched the owner drop off random orders right at the printing press. Nor was there any organized inventory system. Boxes without labels sat inside the door; nobody knew which order they belonged to.

The process was clearly broken.

How things work in your business—how you *do* things—is a big deal. It's what your people will spend most of their time on. It doesn't matter how amazing your brand and culture are; if you don't have functional processes, your business can't scale.

As in the fast-food restaurant but not the printing company, good, documented standard operating procedures will allow you to increase your capacity, improve customer satisfaction, and become more profitable. When your business is firing on all cylinders, your employees are more likely to enjoy their job.

Every business includes processes and microprocesses— probably tens of thousands of them. Whether it's written down or not, you have a procedure for how you deposit a check, pay an invoice, upload a blog post, interview a prospective employee, evaluate performance, answer the phones, file an expense report—all the "plays" your business might run.

When you document processes, you show the method to your madness. At the same time, you make those processes *less* mad! You're organizing chaos; things get clear, and employees don't have to think about how to do the things that should not require their best innovation skills.

After you make sure you've based your processes on best practices, create sets of instructions that other people can follow to operate in the same way, whether it's designing a website or replacing a sink.

Don't document common-sense and low-risk tasks like taking out the trash, replacing the bottle on the watercooler, or telling people how to turn on their computers. Not only will you clutter the playbook with things that people can figure out for themselves, but you'll also risk insulting their intelligence.

WHAT PROCESSES TO DOCUMENT

You might have already noticed how interconnected the four playbook elements are. In Chapter 4 on the People element,

I recommended an exercise for your team to come up with all the responsibilities for their roles. The size of the list might seem overwhelming. At first, you might think, "Wow. This is going to take me forever!" But here's the thing: not every responsibility needs to be documented. Responsibilities are the "what," and processes are the "how." You'll only go through the trouble of documenting "how" if you have a reason to.

Your job as the company leader is to separate the things that don't need documenting from true processes that need to be fully recorded in the playbook.

The responsibilities list is the starting point for those processes. And in the same way that your team helps to brainstorm those responsibilities, documenting the best practices for business processes is a bottom-up, team effort.

Your list to document will still be long, though, so pace yourself by breaking the project into manageable steps. To figure out what to work on in what order, recall what I shared in Chapter 2:

What is done most often? In your business, is there anything that happens dozens or hundreds of times per day? Start with those most frequent processes because documenting them first helps you to avoid the widespread catastrophe of something being done wrong over and over again.

What is done by the most people? Similar to above, consider what processes are shared by the largest number of people. For instance, if you have twelve people in the same sales role in the company, you're likely to find inconsistent ways of operating. Formalize them first.

Other ideas on where to start:

- What is likeliest to be handed off to someone else soon? Is someone leaving soon or are you hiring additional people to share a responsibility as you scale?

- What is being grouped to form a new role? Are you planning to hire someone to take on some of the workload of several employees?

- What is causing bad reviews or causing you to be unprofitable? Bad reviews on Yelp, Google, or Facebook also signal broken processes that need fixing and documenting.

Or, in some cases, as in a new franchise, you may need to tackle the task of writing down everything all at once.

HOW TO ORGANIZE
YOUR COMPANY'S PROCESSES

Imagine walking into a brick-and-mortar bookstore look-ing for business books with no title in mind. If every book in the store were arranged only in alphabetical order by title or author, you'd be lost. Store organizers understand that, so they group books by category and hang conspicuous signs to help people navigate to the collection they want.

Do the same with the processes in your playbook.

Use the following proven four-tier structure to capture all the content in your business, based on the responsibilities you've already brainstormed. Without a structure from the start, you'll have trouble working with the information, and your team will be as lost as a visitor in that hard-to-search bookstore.

Your *collections* will mirror the unique areas of your busi-ness, such as sales, marketing, HR, finance and accounting, customer support, operations, and IT. Depending on the size and complexity of your company, you may have between five and twenty collections. You could also create collections for business units, large teams, brands, product lines, locations, or any other category that you would use to group knowl-edge in your business.

Within each collection, a single *subject*—like a single book at the bookstore—is an all-encompassing knowledge area you might hand someone who needs to learn the whole thing. For example, "Payroll" is a subject within the "Finance and Accounting" collection.

Within each subject are individual *topics*, similar to chapters in a book. They're the actual procedures. An example of a topic—a procedure—within the subject of "Payroll" might be "Running Payroll." Another could be "Creating Payroll Reports." Each topic has value, it has a clear starting and stopping point, and it can be consumed all on its own, yet it fits within the larger context of the subject.

Within each topic are the *steps* needed to accomplish the procedure. In the "Running Payroll" example, steps might include "Logging into the account," "Selecting the appropriate dates," "Reviewing the time entries," "Ensuring enough balance in the company checking account," and "Submitting it for processing."

This structure works in any format—Word, software, or something else. A collection is a folder; a subject is a subfolder; a topic, a document; and steps, bullet points. A system like Trainual provides navigation elements to help you create these tiers and allows additional formatting options, like video.

Collection: Finance and Accounting

Subject: Payroll

Topic: Running Payroll

Step 1: Logging In

HOW TO DOCUMENT
A PROCESS

Working with thousands of companies over the years, I've refined this simple formula for creating a standard operating procedure. Answer each of these questions about the responsibility or process to be able to thoroughly and clearly document it.

1. **What's the process called?** That might sound too obvious, but if the *name* isn't clear—if it doesn't match what team members expect it to be—no one will be able to find the instructions. Keep names simple and intuitive, like "Replying to Support Tick-

ets," "Extending a Job Offer," or "Sending Out the Weekly Newsletter." I like including a verb in the title, because "Running Payroll" is more indicative of what the process is likely to explain than "payroll" itself would be.

2. **Who owns the process?** Every process should have just one owner whose job it is to keep it up to date (and post the date it's updated), make sure people are trained in it, answer questions about it, and confirm it's getting done right.

3. **What physical or software-based tools are needed to perform this process and where can they be found?** Does it require a blank form or company letterhead? Is there a template for, say, a client presentation? Are there required logins and passwords? Or is background information needed, like a client profile including their order history?

Note that you may need to separately create some basic training for the software tools that your company uses, but write each process with the assumption that the person knows how to use the tool. If you don't, you'll end up with dozens of trainings for the same software package.

4. **How often and when is it performed?** If you're training on the process for answering phone calls at the reception desk, provide useful context, such as whether the phone rings five times a day or five times an hour. This knowledge will help team members determine how much time to allow for this task and plan their schedules in general.

5. **How long does it tend to take?** This is especially useful because it communicates how long you *expect* someone to spend on the process. For creative shops, like web designers, do you allocate two days or two weeks for creating mock designs? To avoid applying unneeded pressure, you might add a range or a mention that the process will go faster with practice. Or, if speed is part of the performance measurement, you've given team members a benchmark to work towards.

6. **How is it measured?** Many processes come with important key performance indicators (KPIs)—numbers that show how good a job someone is doing. For example, a KPI might measure how quickly team members respond to customer-support tickets or the maximum percentage of tolerable waste in a manufacturing process.

Some processes will lend themselves to including in the playbook how they look when they're well done, like a picture of a blog post or a video of a client presentation. And for other processes, it might be useful to show a process done right next to how not to do it.

7. **Why does it matter to the company that it's done correctly?** Understanding this context helps team members buy into learning the process. If they know why the standards matter, they're much more likely to *want* to uphold them and to work like a human being with a heart, rather than like a robot.

8. **Finally, what are the steps?** Make them comprehensive and clear. Break up the steps into manageable chunks of content, no more than the approximate length of a half page of paper (roughly 150–300 words). This helps keep the content on the screen, readable at a glance, rather than requiring the team member to scroll through endless text.

Better yet, whenever possible, incorporate screenshots, videos, or screen recordings. If a picture is worth a thousand words, a video is worth thousands of pictures!

Here's an example of a typical business SOP as it would appear in a playbook:

Process: Candidate Phone Screen

Owner: Sasha

Date Updated: August 1, 2021

Tools Needed: Applicant Tracking System, Zoom, Google Workspace

Frequency: As needed (typically 5 times/wk)

Time Estimate: 30 minutes

Context: A Phone Screen is the first step in our company interview process. We use this process to give each candidate a consistent and fair experience, evaluate their fit for the role, and decide whether they should move on to the next step and meet with our hiring manager.

Steps:

Logging Into the Call

Basic Introductions

Share Agenda and Call Flow with Candidate

Ask General Interview Questions

Record Responses in Applicant Tracking System

Selling the Benefits of Trainual

Discussing Compensation

Rating the Call

Following up with Candidates

Each step in this outline should include a detailed description of how to complete that particular step, including text, screenshots, screen recordings, video, slides, or any other format that most effectively describes how to get the job done. For instance, here is what the "Share Agenda and Call Flow with Candidate" step could look like:

SHARE AGENDA AND CALL FLOW
WITH CANDIDATE

An interview without flow can feel like an interrogation. To make your interview more natural and to put your candidate at ease, start with an agenda and a quick overview. After your intros and small talk, say something like:

Perfect. Let's dive in. Just to frame it up, we'll start off with an introduction. From there we will go into your career transitions, some role-specific questions, and chat more about your ideal next opportunity. Then, I'll obviously save some time to tell you more about working here and this particular role! I'll pass the mic over to you and would love to hear more about how you got started in this field.

In the next step, we'll go through basic interview questions to have in your back pocket.

Here is how this particular process would look inside Trainual, with the "Share Agenda and Call Flow with Candidate" step selected:

A FEW FINAL
PROCESS-DOCUMENTING NOTES

Beyond what a process contains, here are some more things to consider when you create this section.

Because so many people contribute to the process section of the playbook, a common pitfall for a company's first one is inconsistent style: every process they write down looks different from everyone else's. What's more, each contributor has to waste time figuring out that inconsistent look.

You can do better. Maintain professionalism and elevate your brand by making your processes look consistent. Establish a playbook style guide including your brand's logo, typography, and colors, along with a dedicated, consistent layout. Trainual's software includes custom brand styles, so all colors, fonts, and sizes look and feel like your company.

KEEP IT CONCISE AND SIMPLE

Documenting a process is nothing like writing a novel or even an encyclopedia article. The inclusion of unneeded instructions and too much complication makes things hard to follow. Limit each process to its essence and to no more than about two hundred words each. Also limit the amount of time a process takes to learn. If it's longer than ten minutes, try to break up the process into smaller chunks.

MAKE IT INTERESTING

Your content doesn't have to be boring. Even if your processes don't have graphics to help teach them, look for places to introduce them. Specifically avoid an all-text playbook. The more variety you can add, the more interesting you'll make the learning process.

If it's appropriate for your brand, you could even inject some fun into the playbook. If you're familiar with Trainual's brand, you won't be surprised that Cuba Gooding Jr.'s character in Jerry Maguire pops up in many of our sales processes ("Show me the money!"). To make your content more interesting, consider using:

- Graphs to show financial progress

- Webcam videos when you want to be casual and personal

- Screen recordings to demonstrate a software application

- Photos to show scenarios in the real world

- Audio recordings of podcast interviews or important company meetings

- Slide presentations for more graphical content

- Live content from social media feeds

- Embedded content from other applications

- Good old GIFs and memes, to add a little personality (or a lot of Cuba Gooding Jr.).

MANAGING THE BIG PICTURE

When you look at all the processes that exist in your company, you'll simplify their documentation by organizing them into the collections, subjects, and topics where they belong. That'll make it easy to prioritize based on what makes the biggest impact on your business.

Then you and your playbook contributors can use the SOP template in this chapter to concisely teach the best practice of each process and answer likely questions.

A few months after I worked with that chaotic commercial printing business, they started to operate more like that restaurant with an assembly line. Now, every order moves through the building and is processed, produced, packaged, and delivered in a consistent, organized way. That's the kind of finely tuned machine you'll create by documenting your processes.

Once you've invested the time and effort into documenting your profile, people, policies, and processes, you need a plan to hand them off to the people who need them. Having things clearly defined gives you the opportunity to effectively train someone, but it's no guarantee that you will.

You've gotten the knowledge out of your head, so now you need to get it into someone else's. How? That's what you'll explore in the next chapter, as the focus shifts from documenting to delegating.

Before you do, take a look at this list of processes that are commonly documented inside growing businesses.

PROCESSES TOPICS CHECKLIST

Every business has hundreds of unique subjects and topics, organized into collections that make sense for how your operations work. Below, I've listed subjects and topics grouped into possible collections (in bold) that you can expand on as you write the processes for your playbook.

HR

Hiring

- ☐ Recruiting Talent

- ☐ Posting Open Roles

☐ Running Background Checks

☐ New Hire Onboarding

Performance and Compensation

☐ Sending Engagement Surveys

☐ Conducting Self-Reflections

☐ Facilitating Performance Evaluations

☐ Adjusting Compensation

☐ Creating Performance Improvement Plans

☐ Documenting Disciplinary Action

☐ Terminating an Employee

Benefits Administration

☐ Benefits Renewals

☐ Registering for Workers Compensation

Customer Support

- ☐ Responding to Support Tickets

- ☐ Handling Customer Escalations

- ☐ Issuing Refunds

- ☐ Pricing Overrides

Finance and Accounting

Accounting

- ☐ Running Payroll

- ☐ Invoicing Clients

- ☐ Account Reconciliation

- ☐ Collections Process

- ☐ Bank Deposits

- ☐ Handling Cash

☐ Paying Incentives and Bonuses

☐ Drawing from Line of Credit

Monthly Reports

☐ Preparing Statements

☐ Progress Billing

☐ Budgeting

☐ Forecasting

☐ Long-Term Financing

☐ Credit Card Payments

☐ Filing Sales Tax

Marketing

Advertising

☐ Paid Ad Strategy

- [ ] Out of Home Strategy

- [ ] Sending Direct Mail Campaigns

Content

- [ ] Using Brand Guidelines

- [ ] Creating a Content Calendar

- [ ] Posting to Social Media

- [ ] Creating a Guest Post

- [ ] Collecting Customer Testimonials

- [ ] Publishing a Podcast

- [ ] Video Editing

Website/Online

- [ ] Managing Our Blog

- [ ] Responding to Online Reviews

☐ Managing Affiliate Program

Marketing Data

☐ Reviewing Google Analytics

☐ Keyword Research

Event Planning

☐ Planning Trade Shows and Events

☐ Sourcing Sponsorships

☐ Securing Partnerships

☐ Submitting Speaker Applications

☐ Building Presentation Decks

Sales

Pre-Sale: Managing Leads

☐ Using Our CRM

☐ Phone and Email Scripts

☐ Purchasing Lists

☐ Follow-up Procedures

☐ Creating Estimates

☐ Creating Proposals

☐ Offering Discounts

☐ Volume Pricing

☐ Processing a Sale

☐ Visiting Clients

☐ Creating Sales Decks

☐ Planning Webinars

☐ Hosting Webinars

☐ Standardized Pricing

Post-Sale

- ☐ Customer Support Handoff

- ☐ Upsells and Downsells

- ☐ Managing Contract Renewals

- ☐ Asking for Referrals

IT

Company Support

- ☐ Learning Our Web Stack

- ☐ Accessing/Troubleshooting Wi-Fi

- ☐ Device Troubleshooting

- ☐ Remote Access

- ☐ Help Desk Requests

- ☐ Printing

Company Equipment

☐ Software Maintenance

☐ Hardware Installations

☐ Data Management

☐ Authorized Devices

☐ Purchasing New Equipment

☐ Upgrade Schedule

☐ Firewall and Security

Operations

Meetings

☐ Creating Meeting Agendas

☐ Facilitating Annual Planning

☐ Facilitating Quarterly Planning

Approvals

☐ Decision Approval Process

☐ Purchasing Approval Levels

Business Supplies

☐ Vendor Selection Process

☐ Ordering Supplies

☐ Inventory Management

☐ Office Equipment Maintenance

☐ Packing and Fulfillment

☐ Drop-Shipping

☐ Quality Assurance

Planning

☐ Development Process

☐ Product Roadmap

Office Management

☐ Front Desk Policies

☐ Email Management

☐ Opening Procedure

☐ Closing Procedure

☐ Receiving Deliveries

7

YOUR PLAYBOOK IN ACTION

I f you've taken the feedback from the previous chapters, you've been able to create something that comprehensively represents your business. Now it's time to focus on disseminating that knowledge to all of the people who need it. Easier said than done.

When I volunteered at a statewide healthcare event to provide vaccinations to the public, I learned a lot about how *not* to train people. It was a horrible experience.

I showed up in the parking lot at 5:45 a.m., ready to start my shift. I checked in, grabbed my reflective vest, and waited for further instructions. A few minutes later, a police officer walked over and said, "Come with me." I blindly followed him through some columns and around a fence. Where he stopped, he handed me a flashlight and said, "This is an exit. Don't let anyone in." Then he walked away.

Huh?

All I could do was stand there for the next hour, frustrated by my lack of orientation and training—and totally clueless about how things worked. The frustration only increased as the day degraded into total chaos. For one thing, it turned out that the reason that vaccine seekers were trying to drive in through the exit was that they hadn't been shown where to register. And others were heading out by mistake without their vaccine because they took a wrong turn, which was too easy to do.

Later on, the same officer wanted a break from directing traffic and asked me to cover for him, so I did. A few minutes later, a supervisor yelled at me to get out of the street. Volunteers were not allowed there, I learned only after I'd violated the rule. (I also learned it doesn't work so well to direct traffic from the side-walk; traffic got a *lot* slower. That rule could use some updating.)

I never knew when *I* would get breaks or, when I did, how long they would be. But the worst part was that event participants kept asking me questions I couldn't answer until *nine hours* into my twelve-hour shift. Only then did someone come over to check on me, hand me a Gatorade, and answer my long list. That's the first time all day that I started to feel confident about what I was doing.

I finished my only shift realizing that this chaotic, stressful cycle would repeat itself every day for every volunteer throughout the event. If I'd had the time, I would've created documentation to help other volunteers and participants. *Somebody* needed to.

As a facilitator of playbooks, I couldn't ignore the irony of being a victim of a seemingly nonexistent one. An event as important as this one definitely had best practices in place for how everything should run and where everyone should go. But no one communicated them—at least not to me or to any of the other misguided volunteers I encountered that day.

Stop the madness! Your company might have done a great job of whiteboarding processes, coming up with workflows, and recording best practices. But the reality is, if you don't communicate all of that to the people who need them, it doesn't matter how comprehensive your playbook is—it's useless.

After all the time and energy that you've put into documenting your best practices, your policies, and all the things that make your business unique, it's time to focus your attention on how to actually train your team.

SELL THE VALUE OF
THE COMPLETED PLAYBOOK

Towards the beginning of this book, you learned you need to sell the benefits of the playbook to the people you'll ask to help create it—the playbook pioneers. At that point, you're making a "what's in it for us" case, explaining why "we're" doing it, so employees don't jump to the (wrong) conclusion that you're trying to replace them.

Once the playbook is finished and ready to share, you need to go through a similar process of selling the playbook, but now it's more about fusing it into your culture. Now the argument shifts to "what's in it for me?"—with "me" being each person who helped you build the playbook. It's important that they know why it exists and what it means for them. For example, it's their way to:

- Achieve career growth in the company

- Hand off responsibilities to free up bandwidth to take on new challenges

- Look like a superstar by suggesting new best practices throughout the company

- Proactively anticipate issues before they become emergencies

- Feel comfortable maintaining a great work–life balance and taking some time off because they know someone else can fill in

For new people who join the company, add the original explanation (because, of course, they weren't there at the start of the playbook project when you first explained it!). They'll need to know that the playbook is your way to:

- Get them quickly up to speed on their job

- Help them understand what's expected of them so they can do their best job

- Make sure they're in the right role

- Make sure they're always leveling up their skills

- Invite them into your community and culture

As time passes, your business grows, and your entry-level employees get promoted, they'll need to hand off their former responsibilities to the people they manage. The playbook facilitates their evolution. Make sure to highlight that purpose as you share your playbook so new people realize you're investing in not just the business but also their growth within it.

ASSIGNING THE PLAYBOOK

You might think of "assignment" as homework. I think of it instead as empowerment.

Having documented everything of importance in your playbook, make sure your team members have full alignment on what they're expected to do, and how you'd like it done. At the same time, you'll empower them to take ownership of their area of the business. You'll start to achieve that goal by assigning the content to your team members.

You can assign content in two ways:

By Role. Group certain policies and processes in your playbook (and the subjects and topics that contain them) to apply to a specific "role" in your business. For instance, you could associate all of the payroll examples that we discussed with the "Controller" role in your company.

If you're using a document-based system, you might designate which content goes to which people by creating folders or tags for each role. The challenge here is when certain content belongs to multiple roles (a playbook software like Trainual can help).

By Individual. You can also assign narrow, one-off content directly to the people who need it, as if you were sending email instructions to one person.

As you assign the content (*which gives your team the ability to see it, search it, or collaborate with you on it*), decide whether the material is **required** reading, or for **reference** only.

At Trainual, we assign our employees required content: all policies and job-related processes that are crucial to them successfully performing their job to our standards. Using our software, we capture employee acknowledgments and store the time and date stamp when they review the material, so that they are always up to speed.

Reference-only material includes less imperative company knowledge, like the best places to get lunch near the office. This could still be assigned if it's relevant for only some people (like those who actually work at the office) but doesn't require tracking or completion.

If you can, try to provide access to your playbook's basic training before some new hires start. New employees tend to get so excited about diving into the playbook that more than half of them have completed their first few days of training by the time they show up to work.

A few caveats there, though—hourly wage employees or temp workers might reasonably expect to be paid for time they spend with the playbook before their first day unless you present it as something like this: "Here's some reading material in case you're interested, but you're not expected to read it in advance."

Also avoid sharing anything proprietary before you know someone will actually show up and start work. Through our company's payroll system, new team members sign a confidentiality and proprietary rights agreement as soon as they accept a job offer. Once they sign it, we're comfortable sharing our training content.

DON'T TRY TO TEACH
EVERYTHING AT ONCE

What if you bought a new car and, before you were able to drive it off the dealership's lot, you were forced to read a three-hundred-page manual and then prove your ability to change the oil, replace a tire, and identify all of the possible warning lights on the dashboard? Not only would it waste your time, but it would likely overwhelm and annoy you.

In the same way, you never want to bombard people by asking them to sit down and read the entire playbook—no matter how proud you'll be of it.

Assign new hires only the parts they need to know at the beginning so they can get in the driver's seat as quickly as possible. In their first two days, that includes no more than the culture and history section of the profile, the policies that apply to them, and the people on their immediate team (or your full company if it has fewer than twenty-five employees).

Then in the next few weeks, you can introduce the parts about members of other teams, your products or services, and the basic processes they'll do often. Within a month or two, when they get all that under their belts, they'll be ready for more intricate, less frequent activities. Most businesses expect to get someone fully up to speed within three months, but of course your training timeline could vary depending on the job, your industry, or your expectations.

TRACK AND TEST
THE LEARNING

The playbook enables gradual and comprehensive training as long as people actually use it. So equally as important as sharing it and selling its value is building in accountability: make sure employees have seen the content they need and that they understand it. Cover the first part of that by asking them to sign off on it, and the second part by testing their knowledge.

Tracking

For tracking, and signing off, on training, I mentioned that the Trainual system adds and stores a date and time stamp as each person progresses through the training. But whatever system you use for tracking, you need some way to track what team members have reviewed and when they've reviewed it. The "when" is important so you can hold people accountable for knowing the newest versions of the content, and in many industries or jurisdictions, it is important for compliance or auditing.

Let's say you've created dozens of new sales scripts in the two years since your first reps were trained. There's no way you can expect them to perform at the same level as the people whose training was recent. Every time you update or create content, you need a systematic way to let the affected people know about it, then to make sure they consume it. Confirm they've done so in some sort of a training log. Keep in mind it would be an unscalable nightmare to keep manual track of who you informed, especially if you tend to frequently add or change content.

Testing

One of the most common questions we get at Trainual is, "How do I know that someone isn't just clicking through the content without actually understanding it?"

One way to confirm and reinforce the learning is to include a quiz or check-in at various training milestones. The check-in could be as simple as a multiple-choice question, like, "Which one of the following six items is not one of our core values?" and requiring a certain percentage of correct answers before people can move on. Or it could be a little more elaborate, like asking people to answer questions about a video you gave them to watch. These assessments are meant to be casual, not to cause any undue stress (unlike the formal testing we all endured in high school).

Another way to assess is to mirror real life. Observe people as they execute the process after learning it in the playbook.

As you test the employee, you're also testing the clarity and completeness of the playbook's instructions. The first people you assign the playbook to are like your beta testers.

BETA TESTING YOUR CONTENT

Of course, it would be great if, before you launched the playbook, you were able to run it through many iterations, but most companies don't have that luxury. What's more typical is trial and error—drafting a process over the weekend, handing it to the person you need to train on Monday, and hoping for the best. If that person has any questions or problems, you can modify the instructions on the spot. Every person you train helps to improve the playbook for the next person.

While you're at it, make sure your people know they're the first to try out this thing and if it doesn't work, it's not their fault. Creating the playbook will always be a team effort and the newest people to receive your training will be the next people to create it.

Scale determines what content should get tested. In most cases, testing will happen organically and informally. When something doesn't go well when someone uses the content, they let the owner know about it, and it gets adjusted. But if you're planning the training for a thousand or more people, invest in the effort of making sure it works before you end up with all those people doing the wrong thing.

For example, IRONMAN® uses our software to train thousands of volunteers—and a staged approach to test it. When we started working with them they tested the training internally with a few people. Next, with a few tweaks here and there, they tested at an actual event. At this point, they're confident about using the material thousands of times over.

LEARNING VS. DOING

If you've written your processes correctly, it shouldn't take long for each employee to outgrow their need for instructions to *do* those processes correctly. After a reasonable number of times in which they need to carefully read one process step at a time (the learning phase), doing the thing should become so automatic that they're able to take off the training wheels. So should you.

Early in my video company, I read *The Checklist Manifesto* by Atul Gawande, and committed to making checklists for everything we did. Checklists are a great starting point as you begin to outline your standard operating procedures (as you see in this book). But there's a risk with checklists, and it comes if you insert them into your task management system, and you start to micromanage every task that your team does.

Don't make the mistake of some companies that expect trained team members to follow extensive checklists as they perform every task. Not only do those companies overwhelm their team members but they clearly communicate their lack of trust in them. The job of playbook processes is to teach, not to let you look over their shoulders every time they do a thing. Once people are trained, checklists actually slow them down and can interfere with their ability to develop better ways of doing things.

Show someone exactly how to do something, and make sure your processes are fully documented, easily accessible, and available for reference when needed. Once you are confident that they know how to do their work, you can stop assigning tasks and rely on them to do the job at hand *without* a checklist. Demonstrate your trust in them, and let them create their own tasks.

WHAT EMPLOYEES NEED TO THRIVE

To make your playbook work in the real world, not just in theory, writing it is not enough. It's also your job to design an experience around how you share the playbook with your people. Promote its benefits, get them up to speed quickly, check in with them along the way, and make sure they understand the material.

If the people at the outdoor vaccination site had shared information that clarified my role in the broader context, I would have been much likelier to encourage my friends to volunteer. The event organizers would probably have attracted more volunteers. At the very least, they would have provided a better all-around experience for the ones they had. That's the power of a welcoming training experience. It can mean the difference between team members who just punch the clock versus those who actually care about what they're doing.

How do you keep your playbook from getting stale and obsolete? You'll find out in the following chapter.

8

NO PLAYBOOK LASTS FOREVER

O f all my consulting experiences, the most memorable one took place at a manufacturing company that had called me in to streamline their front-office processes. The owner of the hundred-year-old family business was giving me a tour when we came to a room with shelves filled with neatly organized and labeled three-ring binders.

These binders—one for every department—contained the company's SOP manuals. There were so many, looking so uniform, that they reminded me of the encyclopedia set my family used to have. As I pulled a binder off the shelf to take a look, the negative space in a thick layer of dust defined exactly where it had been. So, what I found on the cover page should have come as no great surprise to me, but it did anyway: "Last updated March 1989"...untouched for literally decades before my visit!

It was clear that the company had put those books together way back when they were ready to scale—a feat that most businesses never achieve. But having gone through the effort of compiling all that knowledge, they stuck it on a shelf and forgot about it for decades.

When I expressed my shock, the owner made excuses about how the binders were just there for show. Newer processes were on their intranet, he said. Later I learned that those were hardly any more recent. The whole project was frozen in time.

You can't just create a playbook and expect it to stay up to date on its own.[4] Part of your job is building an intention and a culture of keeping it updated. Unlike some three-month goal you check off and move on to other things, a playbook is never finished. As long as your business is changing—presenting new products or services, hiring people, and creating best practices—the playbook needs to change along with it.

And your business had better be changing or it probably won't last too long.

---

4 At least not as of this writing! Our product vision is that someday the playbook will write itself. As the product gets smarter, we'll use AI to detect when something is outdated and to write for you behind the scenes.

WHO SHOULD REVISE?

If your business is big or complex enough to involve delegating the playbook's creation, you also want to delegate its updating.

In a previous chapter, you learned that every process and policy has an owner who's accountable for its compliance and correct execution. This is the person that employees would go to with questions or when something isn't working properly.

Just to clarify, being responsible for doing a process doesn't necessarily mean that person is its owner. For example, every sales rep at your company may be responsible for knowing how to close a sale. But it's the sales manager who's held accountable for the results and improving the process. That's who owns the process.

Of course, the original owner might be promoted or leave your organization between the creation and the updating of that playbook section. In that case, substitute a new owner.

Each owner is also the one who should be ultimately responsible for the update of that process or policy. Before you share your playbook with someone new, the content owners should make sure it still reflects how you want things done. Otherwise, you run the risk of having to retrain a new employee in the same process quickly after they learned it, which isn't a great way to build their confidence in and respect for their new workplace.

But do take advantage of their fresh eyes. The best opportunity for revision is any time you teach part of the playbook to someone new. So not only should you tell every new hire that part of their responsibility is to help you improve the training materials in the playbook, but also tell them how you expect them to do it: by asking questions any time they're confused and by pointing out any inconsistencies between the playbook's instructions and what they hear or observe.

Maybe you, like many companies, have just gotten started with your playbook, and so far, it consists of just a Google Drive of random files. Again, don't throw everything at a new hire or you'll overwhelm them, but you could ask them to take on the project of sifting through the files and setting aside the ones that matter to them in their new role. Here, you're taking ownership of the fact that your training is mid-overhaul, but you're also chipping away at the effort and getting your new hire actively involved.

HOW OFTEN TO REVISE?

When I said a playbook is never finished, your first reaction might have been, "It's hard enough to create a playbook in the first place. Now you're telling me I also have to keep it up to date? What have I just signed myself up for?!" So, it might comfort you to know you'll update only on an as-needed basis, and never all at once.

Think of updating your playbook like maintaining your car. The mechanic doesn't replace every part at once. They'll change the oil and the windshield wipers more frequently than the engine belt. Same thing with your business: some things will need to change more frequently than others.

If your company is growing modestly—you haven't entered new markets, opened new locations, or hired more than five people last year—you might not have to go through all of your content more than once a year. (Well, you might just take a glance at some of it before each new hire starts.)

Make updating a quarterly exercise if you're hiring six to twenty-five people a year. Step it up to monthly or even weekly if more than twenty-five people join the company annually.

Let's say your business is growing 300 percent a year, you're adding a ton of new people, and roles are subdividing by the week. In this case, your playbook should *constantly* evolve. The comfort here is that you also have plenty of people working on it, and a centralized place to get the work done.

The other thing to know is that if things are changing so quickly in your business that 100 percent of it is obsolete in three months, *stop everything*. You weren't ready to create your playbook in the first place; go back to Chapter 2. But as long as that's not the case, just be aware of update triggers.

MORE SIGNS
IT'S TIME TO UPDATE

Don't let your content get stale. Make sure you remember to update everything that needs it.

First, let's talk about updates and formats: playbook software is always live and built to be updated on the go, so it's a lot easier to manage than the alternatives. By (time-consuming) contrast, with a playbook that consists of printed documents, you're stuck with replacing them every time something changes. Same with digital folders and files. In those cases, it's easy to forget to update something.

Here are a few examples of the types of things that are commonly overlooked when it's time to update:

- any screenshots of a website or software that changes

- the names of people who've left or joined the company or moved departments

- software, such as a replaced project management system

- video files

The ability to do a find-and-replace across everything you've written is really important, which is why a paper playbook is a nightmare to keep updated. Ideally, even any videos that you record have searchable transcripts, so you can isolate what's out of date.

In the previous section, I gave you some rough parameters, but you should really be updating *any* time things change. Those things come in two categories. One is what happens *in* your business—as a result of your actions.

For example, expanding geographically is a big trigger for updating your playbook because of the new people, regulations, processes, pricing, communication methods, and maybe even currencies that can come with expansion. Another trigger is any new product, product feature, or service you roll out, so employees know how to promote, support, and process it. The category also includes things like upgrading or adding physical or digital equipment, which often requires a whole new set of instructions.

It's also a good time to update the playbook when you hire people with more experience than the person who held the job before; you want to capture their contributions.

The other category is the unpredictable, environmental things that happen *to* your business. These are the things you're forced to react to, like the pandemic. When it started, we saw thousands of businesses scrambling to update their playbooks to include remote work policies, safety protocols, health screenings, and additional paid time off.

(In fact, the dozens of free new templates Trainual added to our library to help companies respond to the pandemic were downloaded thousands of times. You can access these templates at thebusinessplaybook.com.)

Environmental pressures also include things like reacting to state or federal laws that could affect your payroll systems or to the sales tactics of an aggressive new competitor. In the second case, you'd start by learning about their positioning, articulate how you're different and better, and share that argument with the team. Or a long-term competitor might lower their pricing from the standard, and you could either match that pricing or defend why you don't. Either way, you need to make sure your team has a unified response, and that should be reflected in your updates.

A CAUTIONARY "TAIL"

Preparation in the playbook can influence the outcome in your company even in response to outside events you could never have anticipated. So will the *lack* of preparation. Stuff can happen at any time: if someone posts something negative on social media about your company—whether it's true or not—the rumor will spread if you haven't responded appropriately.

What comes to mind is the early-2021 story about the man who got a surprise when he poured out his morning cereal: two shrimp tails. The story caught social media on fire after the cereal maker claimed that they had inspected the photo and identified the "shrimp" as clumps of sugar—saying that the man was lying. Such a wrong move. It reflected a painful disconnect between the quality control and social media teams.

Although you can't equip your team with a response to every ludicrous scenario that might come up, you should have a consistent protocol in place for dealing with similar ones. You have reason to be proud if the protocol for a customer response sounds more like "Let me look into this and get back to you quickly" than "That's a lie."

The situation would not have blown up if the social media team had been trained in processes for certain types of situations. If that training didn't make it into the original playbook, it's a job for an update. It might look something like this: "If someone makes a claim that could damage our reputation, never make excuses. Reach out individually to the customer, let them know we'll review the situation, and always positively represent our values."

ROLLING OUT UPDATES

Any time you change your playbook, inform the people who need to know what changed and why it changed. Then (again) get some kind of acknowledgment that they heard you. If you're not using a system that does this automatically, a quick email should work. It might look something like this:

> **Customer support team:** FYI. We're changing our refund policy. Now we'll accept refunds for thirty days, instead of sixty days. We did this because we noticed that people who request refunds have already received two notices of being charged within thirty days. We're not asked to give many refunds after thirty days, but when we are, it's hard on the accounting team because they've already closed the month.
>
> Please reply to let me know you've seen this message.

Then make sure you've got a system for tracking who responded. You could do it with a task- or project-management system where you can create tasks that people can check off. You could also do it manually with a spreadsheet or even tally marks on a piece of paper. But at a certain scale, if you don't have a system that automatically tracks compliance, you'll pull your hair out.

Update your playbook on a regular basis, and like a well-maintained car, your company will run better and last longer. You're giving it the means to thrive. But if instead you let it go, you may as well never have created a playbook in the first place.

When I put my manufacturing client's binder back on that dusty shelf, I told him he should think about what else to put there because those binders were going in the trash. By ultimately upgrading their processes and training, they also improved their quality control, ability to update field reps on product changes, and they sped up both customer response time and new hires' ramp-up time—all of which we documented in a playbook that's been kept up to date ever since.

CONCLUSION

Your small business will stay small if you can't manage to remove yourself from the day-to-day hands-on running of it. You can scale only if you delegate tasks and operations to your team and trust them to deliver. A playbook that documents your processes, policies, and culture is the best way to get your business out of your brain and into theirs.

All small businesses can benefit from a working playbook, but too many never invest the time. Now that you have the tools to collaborate with your team and capture the knowledge and uniqueness that exists in your company, I hope you'll use this book as a roadmap to create a playbook that will do wonders for you, your business, and everyone on your team.

Let me leave you with an example of a successful company—Design Pickle,[5] a graphic-design service platform that began with one entrepreneur filling requests for a handful of customers.

The magic here is that from the beginning, the company built a foundation for scaling by being consistent in how they did *everything*. Signing up customers, teaching them to use the platform, receiving design requests, naming files, delivering completed designs, and storing records of their communications—each process was created, perfected, and then documented in a playbook to ensure consistent future performance.

As the company grew, they codified their core values and built a culture around them. They also developed new policies in response to unexpected problems and in the interest of avoiding others. They kept innovating, kept updating, and developed a team to monitor quality control and regularly improve training.

Six years after the company began with only one employee, they've grown to almost seven hundred employees working three shifts a day in thirteen countries.

---

5 Full disclosure: this is a company I've been fortunate to be able to watch from the beginning as an early partner and current board member.

Maybe you don't want hundreds of employees, but you probably do want extra flexibility and freedom in your life—an income that isn't 100 percent dependent on keeping all the plates spinning. A playbook is your ticket to that freedom.

Every business begins by experimenting with what it does really well. When those experiments gel into repeatable processes, you're ready to hand them off to other people— that's where the playbook comes in. Remember, a playbook is made up of four simple elements: the profile of your business, the people who work in it, the policies that guide it, and the processes that operate it. Your job is to document those four elements.

Your playbook will make new people feel welcome and help them know what's expected of them. It will help your best practices become standard practices. And, if you keep it updated, your playbook will help you scale your business, and empower and develop your team. The best part is that you'll enjoy a better lifestyle with less responsibility for day-to-day operations.

Because you're no longer relying on the institutional knowledge of the people who work there, your business could thrive for generations. You're also ensuring its continued success if you ever decide to sell it.

Don't let the task daunt you: done is better than perfectly done. Documenting even your founding story or mission that your employees can align around is better than documenting nothing. Use this book as a kind of checklist of priorities—just get started, then carve away at it little by little.

However you decide to write your playbook, I'm here to support you:

> If you have questions about how to get started or stories about how your playbook helped your company succeed, I'd love to hear from you. You can reach me at cr@trainual.com.

> For free resources, including webinars, templates, and other frequently evolving content to make it easy for you to document the systems in your business, visit thebusinessplaybook.com.

> If you're looking for a tool that automatically does everything I've talked about in this book and you want to join our growing community of businesses around the world, I encourage you to check out what we're doing over at Trainual.com.

When I think back through my career so far, it's sort of like separating time into BC and AD—Before Creating a playbook, and After Documenting one. There's no question which side worked better. Every business needs a playbook. It's time to create yours.

ACKNOWLEDGMENTS

This book took a while to fully bake. In fact, it's still baking, and if I had waited for it to be perfectly done, I never would have published it.

I started writing it nearly three years ago, shortly after the launch of Trainual and built mostly on the foundations of my consulting experience. I had been writing a collection of lessons and short stories for *Inc.* magazine, and I was in the process of formalizing a program for small-business consultants around the world to get certified in Trainual's product.

So, I thought I'd take a stab at compiling all of the lessons and philosophies into a book. I realized quickly that the book was still writing itself, and that as hundreds of new businesses signed up and used our product each week, my perspective and depth of understanding kept evolving. The book project went on pause, and as I recommend here in the text, I stayed firmly in the "do it" phase, until I was ready to document.

It's been a journey since then.

My journey, and my acknowledgments, have to start with my parents, Kathleen and Ralph. Thank you for supporting my entrepreneurial spark at such a young age, and for buying all the lemonade mix before I understood cost of goods sold (unlimited free supplies!).

Mom, thanks for always being my first Like on Instagram. Dad, thanks for setting a great example and making the six-year-old version of me desperately want a briefcase.

Next comes my brother, Jonathan. When I was learning how to run a business, I learned how to delegate because of you and your eagerness to help. Thank you for sending me back to the drawing board when needed, and reminding me to "do it now," when needed. You've forever changed Trainual's trajectory as my partner here.

Thank you to Lianne, my wife, for the ultimatum that taught me about work–life balance. You had the strength to tell me "I won't be your second priority," and that profound moment inspired me to find a way out of the day-to-day. Your uncon-ditional love and support has been such a constant in this chaotic ride.

To my children, Tripp and Callen: if you pay close attention, I'll be filling your playbooks for the rest of my life.

As the ideas for this book started to crystalize, I have to thank Tamara, Helen, and of course Ronnie for the brilliant ques-tions, clarification, and much-needed structure that turned this text into a reality.

Thank you to Chelsey—you make me the superpowered version of myself. And to Becky—for keeping this project on track.

The lessons and experiences in this book come directly from the last two decades of working with hundreds of amazing team members and consulting clients. Aaron, thank you for giving me the freedom to own a business but no longer work in one. To my earliest clients and some of my oldest friends (Russ, Matt, Jake), thank you for trusting me in your compa-nies and pushing me to grow my own.

To the entire team at Trainual, thank you for working tire-lessly to impact millions of small businesses around the world.

And of course, thank you to all the authors and entrepreneurs who have influenced me, especially Michael E. Gerber, whose foreword in this book was a dream come true.

With movies, the first one is often the best, and the sequels never live up to the original. With books, we get the luxury of updating the original over and over again to keep it relevant. So, expect this to get better with time. Endless thanks to you for following along.

More to come.